DK EYEWITNESS TOP 10 TRAVEL GUIDES

SCOTLAND

ALASTAIR SCOTT

DK

DORLING KINDERSLEY
LONDON • NEW YORK • MUNICH
MELBOURNE • DELHI
WWW.DK.COM

Left **Deacon Brodie's Tavern, Edinburgh** Centre **Pollok House** Right **Stirling Castle battlements**

A DORLING KINDERSLEY BOOK

www.dk.com

Produced by Blue Island Publishing,
London

Reproduced by Colourscan, Singapore
Printed and bound in Italy by Graphicom

First published in Great Britain in 2003
by Dorling Kindersley Limited
80 Strand, London WC2R 0RL
A Penguin Company

ISBN 0 7513 4854 6

Within each Top 10 list in this book, no
hierarchy of quality or popularity is
implied. All 10 are, in the editor's
opinion, of roughly equal merit.

Contents

Scotland's Top 10

**The information in this
DK Eyewitness Top 10 Travel Guide is checked regularly.**
Every effort has been made to ensure that this book is as up-to-date as possible at the
time of going to press. Some details, however, such as telephone numbers, opening hours,
prices, gallery hanging arrangements and travel information are liable to change.
The publishers cannot accept responsibility for any consequences arising from the use
of this book, nor for any material on third party websites, and cannot guarantee that any
website address in this book will be a suitable source of travel information. We value
the views and suggestions of our readers very highly. Please write to:
Publisher, DK Eyewitness Travel Guides,
Dorling Kindersley, 80 Strand, London WC2R 0RL.

Left **Isle of Skye** Centre **Pittenweem harbour, East Neuk** Right **Melrose Abbey**

Left **Calton Hill, Edinburgh** Right **Caerlaverock Castle**

Key to abbreviations
Adm admission charge payable

SCOTLAND'S
TOP 10

SCOTLAND'S TOP 10

TOP 10 **Highlights of Scotland**

Scotland has an overwhelming abundance of natural beauty, hundreds of castles stand proud from its long and turbulent past, and an innate flair for enterprise and travel has endowed the nation with artistic treasures from around the world. The culture remains vibrant today, and there's much to celebrate. Here's a distillation of Scotland's best.

1 Edinburgh Castle
Presiding over the nation's capital, the castle is Scotland's pre-eminent sight, a truly inspirational historical and cultural landmark *(see pp8–9)*.

2 National Gallery of Scotland
An internationally significant collection of paintings, from a select group of early Renaissance masterpieces to works by Rembrandt, Velazquez, Gainsborough, Ramsay and Raeburn *(see pp12–13)*.

3 Royal Museum and Museum of Scotland
Two neighbouring museums, one entirely eclectic, the other taking on Scotland from prehistory to the 20th century *(see pp14–15)*.

4 Burrell Collection and Pollok Park
An immensely pleasurable museum, blending into the surrounding park and bringing together such curious bedfellows as a medieval dining hall and Ming Dynasty Buddha *(see pp16–17)*.

5 Glasgow Science Centre
Glasgow's newest major museum, and a spellbinding array of interactive exhibits, visual enthralment and stimulation aplenty for minds young and old alike. Impossible not to be wowed *(see pp18–19)*.

Map labels: 40 miles 0 km; Port of Ness; Scourie; Tc; Outer Hebrides; Stornoway; Isle of Lewis; The Minch; North West Highlands; Le; Tarbert; Ullapool; Rodel; North Uist; Uig; Torridon; Garve; Inverness; Isle of Skye; Kyle of Lochalsh; 6; Loch Ness and the Great Glen; 7; South Uist; Fort Augustus; King; Kilbride; Armadale; Laggan; Inner Hebrides; Rum; Mallaig; Fort William; Coll; Tobermory; 8 Glencoe; Grampian Mo; Lochaline; Isle of Mull; Oban; Crianlarich; Callanc; Fionnphort; Inveraray; Loch Lomond; Greenock; Alexar; Gla; Clyde; 5; Dunmore; East Kilbri; Arran; Irvine; Brodick; Prestwick; Kilma; Campbeltown; Ayr; Cu; Culzean Castle; 9; Stranraer; New; Ste

Previous pages **Loch Torridon**

6 Isle of Skye

An island of romantic tales and the pursuit of royalty, of strange landscapes and formidable mountain ranges, of castle strongholds and religious communities. Skye is a beautiful, wild and magical isle *(see pp20–23)*.

7 Loch Ness and the Great Glen

Ancient geology scarred Scotland, and the Great Glen is its deepest cut, a swath that splits the land in two. A course of water runs through this great valley, forming charismatic lochs, such as notorious Loch Ness *(see pp24–5)*.

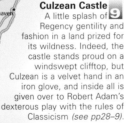

8 Glencoe

To Dickens this was "a burial ground of a race of giants", and, indeed, there is something ominous in the raw terrain of this region. It is a magnificent, sublime landscape, chilled by the history of the bloody 1692 massacre *(see pp26–7)*.

9 Culzean Castle

A little splash of Regency gentility and fashion in a land prized for its wildness. Indeed, the castle stands proud on a windswept clifftop, but Culzean is a velvet hand in an iron glove, and inside all is given over to Robert Adam's dexterous play with the rules of Classicism *(see pp28–9)*.

10 The Cairngorms

Bird lovers, walkers and winter sports enthusiasts praying for snow all head to the woodlands, rivers, lochs, mountains and plateaux of the Cairngorms, the highest landmass in Britain. From ospreys to reindeer to Arctic flowers, it's all here to discover *(see pp30–31)*.

Map labels: so, Wick, Lybster, Helmsdale, North Sea, Elgin, Macduff, Forres, Spey, Huntly, emore, The Cairngorms, Aberdeen, Crathie, Dee, Stonehaven, Pitlochry, Forfar, Dundee, St Andrews, Kinross, Kirkcaldy, Edinburgh, 1 2 3, Dunbar, erwell, Peniculk, Berwick, Peebles, Selkirk, Hawick, Moffat, Dumfries, Gretna Green, Carlisle, Southern Uplands, Perth

🔟 Edinburgh Castle

Dominating the city's skyline as it has done for over 800 years, this castle is a national icon and, deservedly, the country's most popular visitor attraction. Din Eidyn, "the stronghold of Eidyn", from which Edinburgh takes its name, was the vital possession in Scotland's wars. Varying roles as royal palace, barracks, prison and parliament have all helped shape this castle, home to the Scottish crown treasures and the fabled Stone of Destiny.

Beam support, Great Hall

Argyle Battery

🕐 The official tours are wonderful, witty, informative and free. Or you can take a multilingual audio tour, proceeding in whatever order takes your fancy.

🍴 It's rather a limited choice for food at the castle: either The Queen Anne Café in Crown Square (snacks only) or The Castle Café by the One O'Clock Gun for fuller meals.

• Map M4 • Castle Hill
• (0131) 225 9846
• www.historic-scotland.net • Apr–Oct: 9:30am–6pm daily; Nov–Mar: 9:30am–5pm daily; last admission 45 mins before closing • Closed Christmas Day and Boxing Day • Tours every 30 mins • Adm £8; concessions £6; children £2

Top 10 Sights

1. Gatehouse and Portcullis Gate
2. St Margaret's Chapel
3. Argyle Battery
4. Crown Jewels and the Stone of Destiny
5. Royal Palace
6. Great Hall
7. Mons Meg
8. Prison Vaults
9. Governor's House
10. Scottish National War Memorial

1 Gatehouse and Portcullis Gate

The gatehouse was built in 1886–8 more for its looks than functionality. The two bronze statues are of William Wallace and Robert the Bruce *(see pp96–7)*. The original entrance was via the formidable Portcullis Gate of around 1574.

2 St Margaret's Chapel

This tiny, charmingly simple building is the oldest structure surviving from the medieval castle. Probably built by David I (1124–53) in honour of his sanctified mother, it is still used today, and contains some wonderful stained glass *(right)*.

Edinburgh Military Tattoo

3 Argyle Battery

The castle's northern defence offers spectacular views. Don't miss the One O'Clock Gun, fired here every day except Sunday from a great 25-pounder cannon.

4 Crown Jewels and the Stone of Destiny

The UK's oldest crown jewels have lain here since about 1615. However, the fabled Stone of Destiny has been here only since 1996 *(see box)*.

The Edinburgh Tattoo, a military pageant, takes place in the grounds of the Castle in August each year

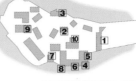

Plan of the Castle

Royal Palace
5 Here in 1556, in a small panelled chamber, Mary Queen of Scots gave birth to James VI, the first king to rule over both Scotland and England.

Great Hall
6 The outstanding feature of this hall is the hammer-beam roof supported on projecting stone corbels. Take time to study all the enchanting little carvings. Constructed around 1500, this is Scotland's oldest wooden roof and probably its most magnificent.

Prison Vaults
8 During the 18th and 19th centuries, the vaults were used to hold French prisoners. Their graffiti can still be seen, as can the objects they made, such as bone dyes for forging bank notes.

Mons Meg
7 A cannon of awesome proportions (below), now housed in the prison vaults. Built in Belgium in 1449, it could fire a 150-kg (330-lb) stone ball over 2 miles (3.5 km) – cutting-edge technology back in the Middle Ages.

Governor's House
9 An elegant and beautifully proportioned house. Alas, it can only be viewed from the outside as it is still reserved for ceremonial use.

Scottish National War Memorial
10 Here is listed all of Scotland's war dead since 1914. Exterior carvings include a phoenix, symbol of the surviving spirit.

Stone of Destiny

According to the mythology that surrounds the Stone, this is the very rock that Jacob used as a pillow when he dreamed of angels ascending to heaven (Genesis 28). For centuries it was kept in Scone Palace, near Perth, and used as the coronation throne for Scottish kings until Edward I invaded in 1296 and carried the stone back to England. For 700 years it was kept under the throne in Westminster Abbey until it was returned to Scotland in 1996.

Scotland's Top 10

For the Top 10 sights on the Royal Mile – the steep thoroughfare between the Castle and Holyrood Palace – **see following pages**

9

Left **High Kirk of St Giles** Centre **John Knox's House** Right **Holyrood Palace**

The Royal Mile

1 Camera Obscura

A great place to start, as this 150-year old observatory has a roving mirror that projects a 360° panorama of the city. It also drops you into a world of illusion and warped images to startling effect. ◉ *Castlehill • Map M4 • (0131) 226 3709 • www. camera-obscura.co.uk • Apr–Oct: 9:30am–6pm daily (Jul–Aug: later closing) • Adm*

2 Writers' Museum

Occupying Lady Stair's House (built 1622) and set in a charming courtyard, this is the place to learn about the three great Scots writers, Robert Burns, Sir Walter Scott and Robert Louis

High Kirk of St Giles

Stevenson, through portraits, manuscripts and personal possessions. ◉ *Lady Stair's Close • Map N3 • (0131) 529 4901 • www.cac.org.uk • 10am–5pm Mon–Sat (Festival: Sun 2–5pm) • Free*

3 High Kirk of St Giles

Often incorrectly called a cathedral, this monumental building has been a landmark and a marvel since 1160. Look for the bagpiping angel (near entrance), the exhilarating rib-vaulted ceiling of the Thistle Chapel and those ancient tatty flags. ◉ *High St • Map N4 • (0131) 225 9442 • www.stgiles.net • 9am–7pm Mon–Fri; 9am–5pm Sat; 1–5pm Sun; Oct–Easter: 5pm closing every day • Free*

4 Historic and Ghostly Tours

A fascinating tour can be taken of Mary King's Close, a medieval street sealed up in 1646 after its inhabitants died of the plague (closed for essential refurbishment work at the time of going to press). Alternatively, choose an adrenalin-pumping ghost tour – evenings are best. Enlightening and fun. ◉ *www.mercattours.com (0131) 557 6464 • www.auldreekie tours.co.uk (0131) 557 4700 • www. witcherytours.com (0131) 225 6745*

5 Scottish Story-Telling Centre

A theatre with a wide range of entertainment, but the insider thing to do here is enquire about the local storytellers. They hold regular and informal meetings,

Writers' Museum

usually in pubs, where anyone can enjoy the "crack" (good yarns). Nothing showy or flamboyant, but real local culture. ◈ 43 High St • Map P3 • (0131) 557 5724 • www.storytellingcentre.co.uk • 9am–5pm Mon–Fri • Free

6 Museum of Childhood

Teddy bears, rocking horses, toy soldiers, castor oil and Lady Penelope – childhood memories come rippling back in the minds of adult visitors. But children find it just as enthralling to see what amused the "oldies" long ago. A remarkable collection. ◈ 42 High St • Map P3 • (0131) 529 4142 • www. cac.org.uk • 10am– 5pm Mon–Sat & 12–5pm Sun in Jul & Aug • Free

7 John Knox's House

Museum of Childhood

The best-known little house in Edinburgh, with its quaint steps up from the street. This was the home of Scotland's fiery religious reformer, John Knox, in 1599. Worth squeezing into for its antiquity alone. ◈ 43-5 High St • Map P3 • (0131) 556 9579 • www.edinburgh.org/things • 10am–5pm Mon–Sat; Jul–Aug: also open Sun 12–5pm • No disabled access • Adm

8 Huntly House Museum

Another medieval house that has battled through the centuries and now houses a specialist local collection, comprising primitive axe heads, Roman coins and all manner of historical finds gathered from the street since the Neolithic Age. ◈ 142–6 Canongate • Map Q3 • (0131) 529 4143 • www.cac.org • 10am–5pm Mon–Sat • Only partial disabled access • Free

9 Scottish Parliament

Spanish architect Enric Mirrales's controversial design of "upturned boats" won the competition for a landmark building for the new Scottish Parliament. Inspired or folly: decide for yourself. Higher up the Mile is the old Parliament House (now the Law Courts). ◈ New Parliament Building Visitor Centre • Map R3 • (0131) 348 6521 • www.scottish. parliament.uk • 10am–5pm Mon–Fri • Free

10 Holyrood Palace

The magnificent royal residence best known for love and murder in the time of Mary Queen of Scots. The state rooms are still used by the current Queen. Climb nearby Arthur's Seat in Holyrood Park for sensational views across town and to the hills and coast beyond. ◈ Map R3 • (0131) 556 7371 • www.royal.gov.uk • 1 Apr–31 Oct: 9:30am–6pm; 1 Nov–31 Mar: 9:30am–4:30pm • Closes irregularly, so check in advance • Adm

The Royal Mile

The city's most historic street runs from the Castle to Holyrood Palace and contains a bizarre mixture of the magnificent and the time-weary. Yet it buzzes with charm and surprises. Congested with street performers during the Festival (see p36), it is a hub of activity and entertainment year-round. Don't try to avoid the melee.

For recommended restaurants and pubs around the Royal Mile, see pp76–7

TOP 10 National Gallery of Scotland

A striking Neoclassical building midway along Edinburgh's Princes Street, the National Gallery defies you to miss it. Widely regarded as one of the finest smaller galleries in the world, this collection is a manageable concentration of excellence. Housed here are works by the greatest names in Western art – Raphael, Titian, El Greco, Rembrandt, Rubens and Monet, to name but a few – as well as the most comprehensive array of Scottish masterpieces. While some galleries tend to intimidate, this one is refreshingly intimate.

The Neoclassical façade

🚌 Throughout summer a special free bus, departing from The Mound, runs between Edinburgh's four principal galleries, including The National.

🍴 A short walk away is a cornucopia of healthy food at the renowned Henderson's Salad Bar, 94 Hanover St.

- Map M3
- The Mound
- (0131) 624 6200
- www.nationalgalleries.org
- 10am–5pm Mon–Sat, 12–5pm Sun (extended during the Festival)
- Free except for special exhibitions

Top 10 Sights

1. Botticelli's *The Virgin Adoring the Sleeping Christ Child*
2. Canova's *The Three Graces*
3. Velazquez's *An Old Woman Cooking Eggs*
4. Raeburn's *Rev Robert Walker Skating on Duddingston Loch*
5. Poussin's *Seven Sacraments*
6. Italian Renaissance Paintings
7. Scottish Painters
8. Classic Portraits
9. The Impressionists
10. Playfair's Building

1 The Virgin Adoring the Sleeping Christ Child

The painting's brilliant range of tones has now been revealed following careful restoration. An unusual Botticelli work for having been painted on canvas and not wood.

2 The Three Graces

One of the world's most famous sculptures, the sisterly trio of nudes was commissioned by the Duke of Bedford in 1815. Canova has all but turned marble into living flesh.

Monet's Poplars on the Epte

3 An Old Woman Cooking Eggs

Velazquez' creation of mood through strong contrast was unprecedented in Spain when he produced this work in 1618.

4 Rev Robert Walker Skating on Duddingston Loch

One of the most celebrated paintings by a Scottish painter. The fun-loving minister depicted is believed to have been a member of the prestigious Edinburgh Skating Club.

Key

■ main floor
■ upper floor

Entrance

5 Seven Sacraments

The seven works depicting the rites of Christianity evoke grand theatricality; they are considered the finest pieces by Nicolas Pousssin, founder of French Classical painting.

6 Italian Renaissance Paintings

Works by Leonardo da Vinci and Raphael stand out. Leonardo's *Studies of a Dog's Paw* show the master's ability to convey a world in a few strokes, while Raphael's *Bridgewater Madonna (right)* is alive with tenderness.

7 Scottish Painters

Look for the superb portraits by Ramsay, Raeburn and Guthrie, and *Pitlessie Fair* painted at the age of 16 by Sir David Wilkie. *Autumn in Glencairn* is an outstanding work by James Paterson.

The Duke of Sutherland

Donations in the second half of the 20th century saw the museum blossom, especially when, in 1945, the Duke of Sutherland presented the gallery with 5 Titians, 2 Raphaels, a Rembrandt and Poussin's *Seven Sacraments*. The works had avoided war damage in London, having already survived the storm of the French Revolution while in the collection of the Duc d'Orleans.

9 The Impressionists

Of the 5 Monets here, *A Seascape, Shipping by Moonlight* is a rare palette knife and brush application, while *Poplars on the Epte (above)* is vintage Monet. Degas' *A Group of Dancers* also features.

10 Playfair's Building

William Playfair chose a Neoclassical style to link Old and New Edinburgh. He also built the neighbouring Royal Scottish Academy and the two buildings have recently been joined.

8 Classic Portraits

The pick of the best must include Rembrandt's world-weary *Self-Portrait aged 51*, Gainsborough's 1777 hit at the Royal Academy *The Honourable Mrs Graham*, and Van Dyck's *The Lomellini Family*, complete with a capering dog. Another favourite is Wilkie's *The Greenwich Pensioner*.

Royal Museum and Museum of Scotland

The best and rarest of Scotland's antiquities have been brought together in two treasure troves. Although they occupy adjacent buildings on Edinburgh's Chambers Street, they maintain separate identities: the Royal Museum concentrates on international artifacts, while the modern Museum of Scotland is dedicated to the story of this land and its people.

1 Lewis Chessmen
These enchanting ivory figures – an anxious king, a pious bishop, glum warriors – were made by Viking invaders in the 12th century.

Museum of Scotland

🕐 Free guided tours daily – check at the main desk.

🍴 The museum's Tower restaurant *(see pp64 & 77)* has fantastic views, or slip round the corner to The Elephant House on 21 George IV Bridge for exotic coffees.

• Map N4
• Chambers St
• Royal Museum (0131) 247 4219
• Museum of Scotland (0131) 247 4422; www.nms.ac.uk
• 10am–5pm Mon–Sat (to 8pm Tue), noon–5pm Sun (for both museums)
• Free

Top 10 Highlights
1. Lewis Chessmen
2. Monymusk Reliquary
3. St Fillan's Crozier
4. The Maiden
5. Bonnie Prince Charlie's Travelling Canteen
6. Natural History
7. Miss Crowford's Shopping
8. Egyptian Toy Mouse
9. Egyptian Mummy Cases
10. The Buildings

2 Monymusk Reliquary
Reliquaries were containers for storing holy relics. This one is linked to St Columba and Robert the Bruce, hero of Bannockburn *(see pp32 & 97)*. It dates back to the 8th century, and although it's tiny, the craftsmanship is exceptional. It is one of the museum's most prized possessions.

Whale skull, Natural History gallery

3 St Fillan's Crozier
Serving as a badge of office, this curved handle was once mounted on a staff carried by St Fillan, an 8th-century Irish monk, active in Perthshire. The filigree ornamentation exemplifies the level of artistry flourishing 1,200 years ago.

4 The Maiden
A grizzly relic to put a shiver down your spine. The Maiden *(left)* was a Scottish beheading machine, similar to the French guillotine, with a weighted blade that descended from on high. It was used in the 16th century.

5 Bonnie Prince Charlie's Canteen

The Prince's cutlery, corkscrew, bottles, cup, and condiments set. Picture the fugitive *(see p21)* in the wild with this lustruous travelling canteen.

6 Natural History

The blue whale skeleton is an ever-popular exhibit, while a glance at the poor dodo shows it to have been, not plump and lazy, but rather athletic, in fact.

7 Miss Crowford's Shopping

The collection of an Edinburgh typist, who spent her lunch breaks browsing for trinkets of glass, shell and plastic.

Museum of Scotland

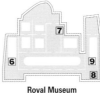

Royal Museum

Key

- Ground Floors
- Third Floor

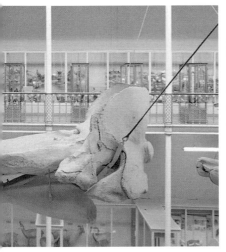

9 Egyptian Mummy Cases

Mummy cases *(right)*, or cartonnages, were made of linen reinforced with resin or plaster and used to contain the embalmed body. Those on display have individually crafted faces and are decorated with ancient Egypt's complex symbolism of death and the afterlife. The cases themselves have already survived 3,000 years.

10 The Buildings

The Royal Museum first opened in 1865 and has been a city landmark ever since. Its cavernous interior and marvellous roof create an extraordinary feeling of light and space. The Museum of Scotland was a custom-built adjunct and has been heralded as one of the most important buildings constructed in post-war Scotland.

8 Egyptian Toy Mouse

It makes you realize how little in the world is new. This pull-along mouse is moulded from brown clay with a stick for a tail. As it moves, the underjaw pivots on pegs and "snaps", while the tail wags from side to side. A treasured toy, and a mere 3,500 years old.

Orientation

Centred on the vast foyer, which helps you get your bearings, the Royal Museum is spread over three floors. Wandering the many halls can be confusing, so pick up a floor plan at the ticket desk. The Museum of Scotland is included on the plan, but its layout is more straightforward as the exhibits are chronological, from Levels 1 to 6.

🔟 Burrell Collection and Pollok Park

The wealth that Sir William Burrell amassed in his lifetime allowed him to indulge his passion for collecting some of the world's finest art, from a wide range of cultures and artistic periods. His hoard (about 9,000 items) constitutes one of the greatest private art collections ever assembled. When he donated it to the city of Glasgow, it was with stringent conditions on how it was to be displayed. The result is breathtaking.

Gallery façade

🟢 The Burrell has a pleasant, if basic, café, with views across the surrounding park.

🟠 On a sunny day, take a picnic and make the most of the park.

- Map U2
- Pollok Country Park, 2060 Pollokshaws Rd, Glasgow
- Burrell Collection (0141) 287 2550; 10am–5pm Mon–Thu & Sat, 11am–5pm Fri & Sun; Free
- Pollok House (0141) 616 6410; 10am–5pm daily; closed 25 & 26 Dec, 1 & 2 Jan; adm £5; concessions £3.75

Top 10 Highlights

1. Hutton Rooms
2. Ancient Civilizations
3. Hornby Portal
4. Stained Glass Collection
5. Tapestries
6. Chinese Ceramics
7. Oriental Art
8. Medieval European Art
9. Old Master Paintings
10. Pollok House and Park

1 Hutton Rooms

Sir William and Lady Burrell did not simply collect art, they liked to live with it. The Hutton Rooms near the entrance of the Collection include an exact reconstruction of the dining room at their home in Hutton Castle, with carved panels from the 15th century and priceless tapestries.

2 Ancient Civilizations

A superb round-up of artifacts from the Sumerian, Babylonian, Assyrian, Persian, Egyptian, Greek and Roman cultures. Don't miss the wicked eye of the cockerel preserved in a Roman mosaic.

Bible Tapestry, 16th century

3 Hornby Portal

More than just a doorway, the portal *(left)* is almost an entire castle wall of 16th-century heraldic carvings, removed from Hornby Castle. It was the largest object Burrell collected and has been superbly incorporated into the structure of the building.

4 Stained Glass Collection

One of the gallery's special surprises is its 600 panels of medieval stained glass. The delight is in the detail for, aside from common religious themes, these panels also give a fascinating glimpse into everyday life in the Middle Ages. Spot the man warming himself before a fire.

Tapestries
5 Burrell justly considered his 150 tapestries to be the most valuable part of his collection. They once hung in the most powerful courts in the world. Look for the enchanting *Bible Tapestry (below)* from 16th-century Germany and the incredible narrative, *Scenes from the Life of Christ and of the Virgin* (c.1450).

Chinese Ceramics
6 Chinese ceramicists are masters in the depiction of movement, colour and expression. Good examples are the Tang dynasty horse *(left)*, stiff with fear, the pouncing lion roof tile and the exuberance of the storks on an enamelled Guan jar. As well as these great works, you'll see writhing dragons galore.

Key
- Ground Floor
- Mezzanine

Entrance

Oriental Art
7 This section covers an astounding diversity of material, from Chinese jades to Near Eastern carpets. Make sure you see the humorous Japanese prints, such as *Shoki The Demon Queller*, and the fine Central Asian embroideries.

Medieval European Art
8 Art was almost exclusively religious in this period, and the Burrell has exceptional ecclesiastical sculptures from European churches. Equally arresting is a 15th-century *Book of Hours*, made for a Breton lady.

Old Master Paintings
9 The star exhibits are Rembrandt's 1632 *Self-Portrait* as a moustached youth, and Frans Hals' *Portrait of a Gentleman* (1639), which was Burrell's most expensive buy.

Pollok House and Park
10 Don't ignore neighbouring Pollok House, which has one of Britain's best collections of Spanish paintings and is set within a beautiful and extensive park *(below)*.

Burrell and the 1983 Building
Sir William Burrell (1861–1958) was a shrewd, wealthy shipowner. He started collecting works of art and antiquities in earnest from 1916, always with a keen eye on price. Such were his demands for the display of his collection that it took Glasgow City nearly 20 years to satisfy them. The award-winning building, finished in 1983, is now considered a work of art itself.

Glasgow Science Centre

This £75-million millennium project is a pure delight. The heart of the centre is the Science Mall, a glass-sided silver balloon with three floors of hands-on experiments, demonstrations and special-effect theatres. Adjacent to this is the world's only revolving tower and an IMAX theatre projecting gigantic 3D films.

Van de Graaff generator

View from across the quay

Check the foyer blackboard for the times/venues of special events. Some have limited places, so get in early.

The Science Mall café serves adequate food, and the ice cream is sensational.

- Map U1
- 50 Pacific Quay
- (0141) 420 5010
- www.gsc.org.uk
- 1 Apr–31 Oct: 10am–6pm (Tower & IMAX: last entry 8pm Thu, Fri & Sat); 1 Nov–31 Mar: 10am–5pm (Tower & IMAX: last entry 7pm Thu, Fri & Sat)
- Adm: IMAX £5.50 (child £4); Tower £5.50 (child £4); Science Mall £6.50 (child £4.50)

Top 10 Sights

1. Tower
2. IMAX Theatre
3. Planetarium
4. Science Show Theatre
5. Science Mall One
6. The Lab – Hands on Science
7. Virtual Science Theatre
8. Science Mall Two
9. Science Mall Three
10. The Buildings

Tower
The entire 100-m (300-ft) tower slowly revolves about its vertical axis. A lift hastens you to the stratospheric gallery for an exhibition on the future of city development and unrivalled views of Glasgow. Delayed by technical troubles, the tower should open in 2003.

IMAX Theatre
Scotland's largest film screen (28 x 20 m / 90 x 65 ft) is found here, showing both 2D and 3D films, including tele-transporting experiences such as *Into the Deep*, *Human Body* and *Everest*. Phone for the latest showings.

Planetarium
When the lights go down, the celestial bodies appear overhead. A spectacular tour unfolds, with individual constellations isolated and identified, culminating in the whole night sky over Glasgow being shown as it is beyond the city's light pollution.

Science Centre

Science Show Theatre
Science graduates take turns to give witty and informative demonstrations. Burning gases, flying projectiles and various magical effects are produced and explained.

Science Mall One
5 Handles to turn, buttons to press and lots to be learnt about light, energy and our bodily senses. A special area designated for the very young includes a fabulous walk-on piano.

The Lab
6 Here children get the chance to sit at lab tables and be guided through such formative experiments as making their own toothpaste.

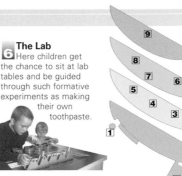

Key

◼	Ground Floor
◼	1st Floor
◼	2nd Floor
◼	3rd Floor

Virtual Science Theatre
7 Don 3D glasses and enter a stream of virtual worlds, from the ins and outs of car design to trainee surgery (not as grizzly as it sounds) and on to a city in Sweden that has recreated itself in digital form.

Science Mall Two
8 Highlights here are: the microscopy lab, with live fruit flies; the construction area, where you can build bridges; and the biotechnology lab, which provides a look inside your own body.

Science Mall Three
9 The environment features here, and you have to make global decisions. There's also a section on the human organism and opportunities to design a baby or change sex – virtually, of course.

The Buildings
10 Take time after your visit to stroll around the buildings and interactive fountain, and savour the radical design. Also, over the Clyde you'll see the derelict docks, once the site of Glasgow's formidable shipping industry.

Science in the Dock

Where is science leading us, and should we be concerned? A daring and brilliant presentation alerts us to a sense of global as well as individual responsibility. An animated theatre presentation explores moral dilemmas surrounding issues such as the first heart transplant and the cloning of Dolly the Sheep (see p35). Ideal for all ages; 3rd Floor.

Isle of Skye

The product of violent geographical upheavals, the "misty isle" is justly famed for its towering, ragged mountains and wild coastline. Add to these a colourful patchwork of crofts (farms), waterfalls, an exceptional whisky, a castle linked to the fairy world and the historical romance of Bonnie Prince Charlie, and you find on Skye all the ingredients that best symbolize the Highlands.

Flora MacDonald's headstone

Old Man of Storr

🔊 The Aros Centre has evenings of Gaelic culture – no hackneyed shows but the best of local talent.

🍴 The Sligachan Hotel is central and does great bar meals – good atmosphere and a play area for kids.

• Map D2
• Aros Centre, Portree (01478) 613649; www.aros.co.uk; free
• Talisker Distillery, Carbost (01478) 614308; Easter–Oct 9:30am–5pm Mon–Sat; rest of year 2–5pm Mon–Fri; £4 for tour
• Dunvegan Castle (01470) 521206; Open daily; adm £6
• Loch Coruisk Boat Trips, Elgol (0800) 7313089; Apr–mid-Oct
• Armadale Castle (01471) 844305; Apr–Oct: daily; adm £4.50
• Skye Museum of Island Life (01470) 552206; www.skye museum.co.uk; Easter–Oct: daily; adm £2

Top 10 Sights

1 Aros Centre, Portree
2 Portree
3 Talisker Distillery
4 Dunvegan Castle
5 Quiraing and the Old Man of Storr
6 Loch Coruisk
7 The Cuillins
8 Armadale Castle Gardens and Museum of the Isles
9 Skye Museum of Island Life
10 Island of Raasay

1 Aros Centre, Portree
An exceptional visitor and arts centre, created by locals with a passion for their culture. The place to learn about Skye's history and places to visit.

2 Portree
Portree *(above)* is Skye's mini capital, with some excellent shops and a delightful harbour lined by colourful buildings. Sailing races and Highland Games are big events in summer.

Loch Coruisk

3 Talisker Distillery
"The lava of the Cuillins" is produced at Skye's only distillery, where visitors are welcomed onto a friendly tour.

4 Dunvegan Castle
Home to the chiefs of Clan MacLeod for 1,000 years. Here, you'll see the Fairy Flag, which, it is said, can rally the "little people" to protect the clan.

5 Quiraing and the Old Man of Storr
A fantastic region of cliffs and pinnacles *(above)*, one rocky outcrop gaining the name the Old Man of Storr.

6 Loch Coruisk
The boat from Elgol passes seal colonies to reach this secret loch, trapped in a bowl beneath the Cuillins, where a prized view awaits.

7 The Cuillins
This awesome range rises from the sea to almost 1,000 m (3,300 ft). The Black Cuillins are a challenge even to seasoned climbers, but the Red Cuillins are an easier prospect for walkers.

8 Armadale Castle Gardens and Museum of the Isles
Beautiful coastal gardens surrounding the ruined castle of clan MacDonald, with a historical archive.

9 Skye Museum of Island Life
Delightfully evocative, this reconstruction of thatched cottages, or "black houses" (they were blackened by firesmoke, *below*), turns back the years a century or more.

10 Island of Raasay
Its beauty too often overlooked, Raasay offers land and watersports at its Outdoor Centre, or you can climb Dun Caan to where Johnson and Boswell, the celebrated 18th-century men of letters, famously danced a jig.

Flora MacDonald

"Bonnie Prince Charlie" was pursued relentlessly by government troops following his defeat at Culloden. He escaped to Skye disguised as maidservant to the courageous Flora MacDonald. She was imprisoned for this act. On her release she emigrated to America, but later returned to Skye, where she died in 1790, one of the Prince's bed sheets providing her burial shroud.

Scotland's Top 10

For great walks on Skye, **see following pages**

21

Left **Old Man of Storr on the Trotternish Ridge** Right **Elgol**

TOP 10 Walks Around Skye

1 The Cuillins
Of the two Cuillin ranges (the red and the black), the Black Cuillin Ridge is perhaps the most magnificent range in Britain, a craggy backbone 8 miles (13 km) long with over 20 peaks classed as munroes *(see pp40–41)*. Traversing this range represents a tough two-day challenge for serious rock climbers. But there are easier walks in the Red Cuillins (formed from red sandstone), which offer magnificent views. Try a walking ascent of Glamaig (775 m / 2,500 ft), near Sligachan.

2 Trotternish Ridge
A spectacular escarpment walk, with sections that seem to evoke moonscapes. For an easy day walk, drive from Staffin towards Uig and stop at the hilltop car park. From here, take the path north and walk to the Quiraing, the area of the best pinnacles (a 2-mile / 4-km round trip). For an even better experience, take a tent and walk the entire ridge.

3 Neist Point Lighthouse
Another short walk (only about a mile / 2 km in total), but a coastal path this time. Take the lovely road to Waterstein on the Duirnish Peninsula and park where the tarmac ends. From here, it is a gentle, relatively level stroll to Neist Point Lighthouse. Great views of the cliff-edged coastline and usually plenty of seabirds, as well as the odd seal.

4 Sligachan to Glenbrittle
This walk passes below the Black Cuillins and alongside the Allt Dearg Mor river, which has many waterfalls. The path is boggy in places but generally good, and the gradients are easy if walked from east to west (starting at Sligachan). It's best

Hill walker in the Cuillins with Loch Coruisk below

Note: always wear appropriate clothing, take supplies of food and water and check the weather report before setting out

to arrange in advance for a lift back from Glenbrittle.

5 Armadale Castle Forest Walks

Skye is not noted for its trees, but the exception is the region of Sleat, the "garden of Skye", and Armadale Castle in particular. Aside from

On the path to Loch Coruisk

short walks within the castle's spacious gardens, a series of forest trails leads up to the Old Farm and the Hilltop Viewpoint. These are lovely leafy trails, and the peak offers a panoramic vista over the sea.

6 MacLeod's Tables

These two flat-topped (hence the name) hills on the Duirnish Peninsula are not hard to climb, but there are no paths and the going can be a bit rough and boggy in the lower reaches. Healabhal Bheag, the slightly taller southern hill (500 m/ 1,600 ft), is the easier of the two to ascend, and best approached from Orbost, to the east. Splendid views from the top. It's about 4 miles (7 km).

A walker on Skye

7 Dun Caan, Isle of Raasay

Another distinctive flat-topped hill, this time on Skye's slender neighbour, the Isle of Raasay. In 1773 the famous literary duo, Samuel Johnson and James Boswell, walked up here to enjoy the scenery; they enjoyed it so much, in fact, that they danced a jig. Given Johnson's bulky physique, that would have been some sight. Nevertheless, the story illustrates the powerful allure of Raasay. 3 miles (5 km).

8 Fairy Glen

On the south side of Uig town a small road leads inland for 2 miles (4 km) to an area of knolls, hillocks and dells known as the Fairy Glen. There are sheep paths among all these grassy formations: follow them to wander this enchanted glen. It is easy to see how the area got its name, and this is a fine spot to enjoy a leisurely picnic.

9 Elgol to Loch Coruisk

This is a long walk: about 10 miles (16 km). A map is essential, and a tent advised (or return by boat – *see p20*). The coastal track is rough but delightful, and Camasunery has a fine beach. On the last stage, take great care on The Bad Step. The destination, Loch Coruisk, is divine.

10 Boreraig and Suisnish

These are two ruined villages whose inhabitants were cleared for sheep. The best is Boreraig, accessible by rough walking from Heaste (about 5 miles / 8 km). It also has a fine waterfall and pool for swimming. Alternatively, you can do a round trip (twice the distance) from Torrin and take them both in. The track is good in places, no more than a sheep trail in others.

To undertake these walks, you will need a large-scale walking map. For map recommendations, see p132

TOP 10 Loch Ness and the Great Glen

A geological rift split the land from coast to coast, once dividing Scotland in two. Glaciers deepened the trench and the result today is a long glen of steep-sided, wooded mountains and dark, mysterious lochs. Castles and forts abound, bearing witness to the Great Glen's strategic importance and enhancing its dramatic grandeur with intrigue and nostalgia. And, of course, there's the legendary Loch Ness monster, elusive but irrepressible, and still attracting scientific interest – keep that camera to hand.

Urquhart Castle

The best way to experience Loch Ness is by boat. Regular cruises leave from Inverness and tour as far as Urquhart Castle.

Quality food upstairs, good pub below, at the Lock Inn, Fort Augustus.

- Map D4 & E3–D4
- Aonach Mor Ski Gondola, (01397) 705825; Open daily • Jacobite Steam Train (01463) 239026; Jul–Sep daily
- Jacobite Cruises (Canal and Loch Ness) (01463) 233999; 25 Mar–Oct
- Great Glen Watersports Park (01809) 501381 • Urquhart Castle (01456) 450551; 9:30am–6:30pm daily; adm £5 • Official Loch Ness Monster Exhibition, Drumnadrochit (01456) 450573; Easter–Sep 9am–7pm daily; rest of year 9am–5pm daily; adm £3.50 • Fort George (01667) 462777; 9:30am– 6:30pm daily; adm £5

Top 10 Sights

1. Fort William
2. Loch Lochy
3. Caledonian Canal
4. Great Glen Watersports Park
5. Fort Augustus
6. Glen Affric
7. Urquhart Castle
8. Loch Ness
9. Inverness
10. Fort George

1 Fort William
Close to Glencoe and at the foot of Britain's highest mountain, Ben Nevis (1,343 m; 4,406 ft), this seaside town provides an ideal base for walkers. The scenery is faultless, and almost every direction offers enticing terrain. The less active can scale Aonach Mor by ski gondola or take the Jacobite Steam Train to Mallaig.

Urquhart Castle

3 Caledonian Canal
An outstanding feat of construction, engineered by Thomas Telford and connecting lochs Ness, Oich, Lochy and Linnhe. Watch boats glide past at Fort Augustus.

2 Loch Lochy
A path on this splendid loch's northern shore is now part of the Great Glen Walk and cycleway. Look out for the wonderful Cia Aig waterfall on the road to Loch Arkaig.

4 Great Glen Watersports Park
A sensitively landscaped centre among trees on Loch Oich, the smallest and most secluded in the glen. Sail, swim, windsurf, canoe, water-ski, fish or shoot the rapids on a raft.

24   For Glencoe, the spectacular region near the southwestern end of the Great Glen, see pp26–7

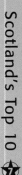

5 Fort Augustus
A delightful village on Loch Ness. Take a sunlit evening walk in the grounds of the former abbey-school built in grand style in 1878.

6 Glen Affric
A lovely forest road leads to this renowned beauty spot. From here, a two-day hike can take you to the west coast.

7 Urquhart Castle
Magnificently situated on the edge of Loch Ness, these ruins were formerly one of Scotland's largest castles. A fine tower house still stands, and the views from the top are well worth all the climbing. The visitor centre is state-of-the-art and displays a huge array of medieval artifacts.

8 Loch Ness
With a depth of almost 300 m (1,000 ft) and unusually black water, this immensely atmospheric loch is Scotland's longest at 26 miles (42 km). Flanked by mountains, castle and abbey ruins, and several charming villages, Loch Ness is worthy of its fame. Take the north road along its bank.

9 Inverness
The "Capital of the Highlands", Inverness is a bustling shopping centre set below a pink Victorian castle. The emotive battlefield of Culloden is nearby and the visitor centre there revives this sad and poignant event (see pp32–3).

10 Fort George
Built in the aftermath of Culloden on a sandy promontory on the Moray Firth, Fort George (below) is the mightiest artillery fortification in Britain. It's still in use as a barracks today, and has only ever undergone minor modifications.

Tales of Nessie

First recorded by St Aiden in the 7th century, "Nessie" pops up time and again. Despite many hoaxes and faked shots, there's still a convincing body of sonar and photographic evidence to support the existence of large creatures here, and scientific opinion remains open. To decide for yourself, visit one of the Loch Ness Monster Centres in Drumnadrochit, which present the evidence.

Glencoe

Nowhere else is the traveller confronted so abruptly by the arresting impact of Scotland's mountains. The road twists below the towering bulk of these characterful peaks, sometimes dark and louring, sometimes light and enticing. This ancient and celebrated pass is also imbued with history: cattle rustling, clan feuds and – most notoriously – the "Massacre of Glencoe" in 1692. In summer the area is a favourite haunt of walkers and climbers; in winter it is one of the leading ski resorts.

Rannoch Moor

🚗 Drive (carefully!) the narrow scenic road that runs parallel to the main A82 from Glencoe Village to the Clachaig Inn.

🍴 The craft shop in Glencoe village has a good menu in a bright and bookish atmosphere. The desserts are delicious.

• Map E3
• Glencoe Visitor Centre (01855) 811307; May–Oct: 10am–6pm daily
• Scottish Sealife Sanctuary (01631) 720386; www.sealsanctuary.co.uk; Mid Feb–Nov; adm £6.75
• Confectionery Factory (01855) 821277; Open daily; Free
• Aluminium Story (01855) 831663; Apr–Sep: 10am–5pm Mon–Fri (closed 1–2pm); donations
• Glencoe Ski Centre (01855) 851226; Jan–Apr & Jul–Aug; skiing day pass £20; summer chairlift £4

Top 10 Sights

1. Glencoe Visitor Centre
2. Signal Rock, Glencoe Memorial and Forest Walk
3. Invercoe Loch Walk and Pap of Glencoe
4. Loch Leven
5. Views of the Three Sisters
6. Devil's Staircase
7. Glencoe Ski Centre
8. Rannoch Moor
9. Scottish Sealife & Marine Sanctuary
10. Castle Stalker

1 Glencoe Visitor Centre

This centre *(below)* possesses a superb exhibition and audio-visual presentation – allow an hour to take it all in. If you're walking, a satellite weather report for the area is regularly updated.

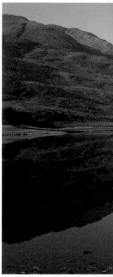

Glencoe from Loch Leven

2 Signal Rock, Glencoe Memorial and Forest Walk

A series of enchanting forest trails leads to the Signal Rock lookout, where the MacDonalds would light fires to send messages to other clan members.

3 Invercoe Loch Walk and Pap of Glencoe

A particularly beautiful loch, especially in May when its rhododendrons are in full bloom. Behind looms the distinctive peak the Pap of Glencoe, its isolation affording panoramic views.

For suggested walks around Glencoe see pp40–43

4 Loch Leven

The drive round this scenic loch *(left and below)* is punctuated by a confectionery factory and an exhibition on Kinlochleven's aluminium industry.

5 Views of the Three Sisters

By a bend in the main road and next to a roaring waterful is a rocky knoll known as "The Study", a fine viewpoint for this trio of similarly-profiled sibling mountains *(below)*.

6 Devil's Staircase

A tortuous section of the West Highland Way *(see pp42–3)*, offering views to Rannoch Moor and Black Mount. The path continues to Kinlochleven for a greater challenge.

8 Rannoch Moor

A beautiful but boggy wilderness, best seen from a window of the Ft William to Tyndrum train.

10 Castle Stalker

A dreamlike castle, not open to visitors but magical to see, rising from an island barely big enough to contain it *(above)*.

7 Glencoe Ski Centre

Among the most popular of Scotland's five ski resorts. All the gear available for hire in winter, and the perfect terrain for snow thrills.

9 Scottish Sealife & Marine Sanctuary

The sanctuary's rescued seals can be seen through underwater windows, and many other sea creatures can be viewed in the aquarium. But best of all is the skate and ray pond, where you can touch these tame and elegant swimmers as they glide about.

The Massacre of Glencoe

Having signed an oath of submission to William III in 1692, albeit five days late, the MacDonald clan generously entertained and billeted 130 government soldiers in their homes for 10 days. The soldiers then slaughtered their hosts, leaving 38 dead. As much as the brutality, it was the utter breach of trust that shocked the nation.

TOP 10 Culzean Castle

Formerly a rather dull fortified tower house, Culzean (pronounced "Cullane") was transformed by the architect Robert Adam into a mansion of sumptuous proportions and elegance. The work began in 1777 and lasted almost 20 years, the Kennedy family sparing little expense in the decoration and craftsmanship of their clifftop home. Culzean – a masterpiece in a land full of magnificent castles – was gifted to the nation and fully restored in the 1970s. Its grounds became Scotland's first public country park in 1969.

Castle façade

🔵 It's all too easy to overlook half of the Walled Garden, and so miss the wonderful Victorian Vinery, where period species of dessert grapes are grown under glass.

🔵 Check out the visitor centre restaurant to see if their tasty venison casserole is on the menu.

• Maybole • Map G3
• (01655) 884455
• www.culzeancastle.net
• Late Mar–Oct: 10am–5pm daily; Nov–Dec: 10am–4pm Sat & Sun
• Castle grounds: 9:30am–sunset daily;
• Adm: combined ticket for Castle and Country Park £9, family £22; for Country Park only (including Castle grounds) £4.50, family £12.50

Top 10 Highlights

1. Oval Staircase
2. Armoury
3. Saloon
4. Lord Cassillis' Rooms
5. Eisenhower Apartment
6. Picture Room
7. Country Park
8. Home Farm Visitor Centre
9. Camellia House
10. Clifftop and Shoreline Trails

1 Oval Staircase
Nothing short of perfection *(below)*. Ionic and Corinthian pillars swirl above a strawberry red carpet, lit up by an arched skylight.

2 Armoury
Countless weapons cover the walls in concentrated patterns. The 120 blades forming a star over the fireplace are a fraction of this fearsome arsenal.

3 Saloon
The most beautiful room in the castle, with its bold colours and circle of windows overlooking the sea. Louis XVI chairs sit softly on Adam carpets.

The Castle and its parkland

4 Lord Cassillis' Rooms
Restored to their late 18th-century décor *(below)*. The vivacious wallpaper is Chinese; the four-poster bed late Chippendale.

5 Eisenhower Apartment

A gift to the US president in gratitude for his support in World War II. Not open to the public, but it can be hired.

Plan of Castle

Key

▣ Ground floor

▢ First Floor

6 Picture Room

Formerly the High Hall of the old tower house, this was the first room Adam transformed, and the first to be faithfully restored in 1972 *(below)*.

7 Country Park

Reckoned to be the most magnificent park in Britain, this coastal swath of woodland, ponds, gardens, beaches and clifftop walks retains the park's original character.

8 Home Farm Visitor Centre

No ordinary farm, but more of a fortified village within the country park, now transformed into a visitor centre and café.

10 Clifftop and Shoreline Trails

The views to the mountains of Arran are glorious from these vantage points. Two favourite destinations are Swan Pond and Happy Valley. Free guided tours (about 1 hour) depart from the visitor centre, or go it alone.

9 Camellia House

This impressive baronial greenhouse *(below)* is one of over 40 lesser architectural features found dotted around the grounds. It's a Gothic home for the collection of camellias.

Robert Adam

Born in Kinross-shire in 1728, Adam was educated at Edinburgh University. His subsequent tour of Italy determined his Neo-Classical style, and he went on to set up an architectural practice in London, becoming the foremost designer of his day. A true workaholic, his fanaticism for detail was legendary. Adam died in 1792, the year Culzean was completed.

TOP10 The Cairngorms

The highest mountain massif in the British Isles comprises a magnificent range of peaks, wild lochs and ancient forests, as well as bird sanctuaries, nature reserves and sports amenities. It is a region of exceptional scenery and habitats that have not been divided by roads. Activities take place on its fringe, but the heartland remains open only to those who travel by foot or on skis. It is this relative isolation that makes it so appealing both for the wildlife that inhabits the region and for the people who thrive on the testing terrain.

River Spey

🌀 The Reindeer Centre offers guided hill visits daily at 11am.

🌿 The place to eat is the Old Bridge Inn in Aviemore – innovative blackboard specials and tables by the river in summer.

• Map D4–5
• Cairngorm Mountain Railway (01479) 861261; Open daily
• Cairngorm Reindeer Centre, Glenmore (01479) 861228; adm
• Loch Garten Osprey Ctre; Apr–Aug daily; adm
• Strathspey Steam Railway (01479) 810725; Jun–Oct
• Highland Wildlife Park; 10am–dusk; adm
• Spirit of Speyside Whisky Festival, www.spiritofspeyside.com
• Malt Whisky Trail: distillery opening times and admission costs are listed at www.maltwhiskytrail.com

Top 10 Sights

1. Aviemore
2. Highland Wildlife Park
3. River Spey
4. Loch an Eilean
5. Cairngorm Reindeer Centre
6. Loch Morlich
7. Cairngorm Mountain Railway
8. Strathspey Steam Railway
9. Loch Garten Osprey Centre
10. Malt Whisky Trail

1 Aviemore

Traditionally a dormitory town for skiers as well as the jumping-off point for touring the region at any time of the year, Aviemore consists of a concentration of hotels, guesthouses, bars, restaurants and après-ski (or, indeed, après-anything) entertainment.

Valley in the heart of the Cairngorms

2 Highland Wildlife Park

The once-common bison *(above)*, bears and wolves may no longer roam wild, but you can find them here, along with otters, pine martens and wild cats.

3 River Spey

Scotland's finest salmon river and birthplace of whisky, the Spey is a river of dark pools and fast rapids. It winds through a rich variety of landscapes: moorland, forest, pasture and grainfield.

4 Loch an Eilean

A hidden gem, 5 miles (8 km) from Aviemore. One of Scotland's best short walks is along this loch, nestling below the mountains. Its trees are magnificent, and its crowning glory is an ivy-clad castle.

For suggested walks in the Cairngorms see pp40–43

5 Cairngorm Reindeer Centre

Britain's only herd of wild reindeer *(above)* was introduced to Scotland in the 1960s. These charming animals, now numbering 150, roam free and are very friendly.

6 Loch Morlich

Surrounded by the wonderful Caledonian pines of Rothiemurchus Forest, Loch Morlich is a circle of tranquil water at the base of the Cairngorms.

7 Cairngorm Mountain Railway

This new railway takes you almost to the top of Cairn Gorm mountain. The views are nothing short of sublime, and at the Ptarmigan restaurant you can enjoy the most elevated meal in the country.

8 Strathspey Steam Railway

The train *(above)* chuffs from Aviemore to Loch Garten through a lovely landscape. On weekends there's a special Thomas the Tank Engine up front.

9 Loch Garten Osprey Centre

Ospreys began breeding here in 1954, after a 40-year absence. Vigilance has been necessary to foil egg-collectors, but now more than 2 million visitors have seen the birds from this hide.

10 Malt Whisky Trail

The process of turning water into the "water of life" is a vital part of Scottish culture. Half of the nation's distilleries are on Speyside, and the signposted "whisky trail" leads the way to seven of them *(whisky barrels below)*.

Spirit of Speyside Whisky Festival

A merry May festival in which you can view illicit stills and the Customs and Excise Contraband Caravan, ride The Whisky Train, dance a Highland Fling and cook your own scones against the clock. To the sounds of pipebands, the highlight is an opulent whisky dinner.

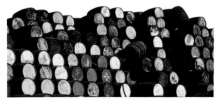

Left **St Columba** Centre **Clyde Docks** Right **Scottish soldiers**

🔟 Moments in History

1 St Columba Founds a Monastery on Iona

In 563 this fiery Irish missionary went into self-imposed exile on Iona. Here he founded a monastery, which became known as the "Cradle of Christianity". Columban monks travelled widely, consolidating the Christian faith and thus unifying Scotland's tribes into one nation.

Battle of Bannockburn

2 Battle of Bannockburn

Facing an English onslaught in 1314, the Scots – led by Robert the Bruce – achieved a dazzling victory. By defeating the English, the Scots won back their nation and their pride. Their right to independence was ratified by Papal bull in 1329, though the war with England continued for another 300 years.

3 Battle of Flodden

To assist France, James IV invaded England in 1513 and met the enemy just over the border at Flodden. In the massacre that followed, 10,000 Scots died, James included, and, as his heir was still an infant, a power struggle and an era of instability ensued.

4 John Knox leads the Reformation

Scotland was a Catholic country when Mary Queen of Scots ascended the throne. But in 1559,

a revolutionary preacher called John Knox fearlessly denounced Catholicism and heralded the Reformation. Protestantism was introduced to Scotland, and for the next 150 years religious intolerance was rife.

5 Union of the Crowns

When Elizabeth I, Queen of England died without an heir, James VI of Scotland (son of Elizabeth's cousin Mary) had the strongest claim of succession. He was crowned James I of England in 1603, and his court was moved to London. Scotland retained its parliament and independence, but would now share its monarchs with England.

6 Union of Parliaments

A disastrous attempt to establish a trading colony in Panama almost bankrupted Scotland, and union with England was necessary for economic survival. The Act of Union (1707) dissolved Scotland's parliament and the politicians moved south.

7 Battle of Culloden

In 1745, James VII's grandson "Bonnie Prince Charlie" secretly sailed from France to Scotland to reclaim the British throne. He amassed an army which fought its way to a panic-stricken London. Short of their goal, the "Jacobites" lost heart and returned north. The Hannoverian army, augmented by royalist Scots, slaughtered the rebels at Culloden, the last battle fought on British soil.

8 Industrial Revolution
James Watt's transformation of the steam engine *(see p34)* heralded the advent of the Industrial Revolution, which had a profound effect on Scotland, and Glasgow in particular. The demand for steam forced every coal mine into maximum output, and the production of cotton, linen, steel and machinery boomed. Glasgow became known as "the work-shop of the Empire".

9 World Wars and Emigration
Of the two world wars, it was the 1914–18 war that claimed the most lives: 74,000 Scottish soldiers and almost as many civilians. In addition to this, between 1901 and 1961, 1.4 million Scots emigrated to seek better lives elsewhere.

10 Re-establishment of a Scottish Parliament
In a 1997 referendum, the Scots emphatically voted for the re-establishment of a Scottish Parliament. This opened in 1999, returning the political forum to the heart of Scotland after an absence of 292 years.

Scottish Parliament

Top 10 Writers

1 John Barbour (c. 1316–96)
The "father of Scottish poetry and history". His epic poem is *The Brus* (1370).

2 Robert Burns (1759–96)
The national poet whose worldwide acclaim has titled him "the bard of humanity".

3 Sir Walter Scott (1771–1832)
The first best-selling author, whose novels and poems launched a romantic tradition.

4 Robert Louis Stevenson (1850–94)
Best remembered for *Treasure Island*, this revered Edinburgh author travelled widely and died in Samoa.

5 Sir Arthur Conan Doyle (1859–1930)
Mastermind behind Sherlock Holmes. He was born in Edinburgh and trained as a doctor.

6 J M Barrie (1860–1937)
Born in Kirriemuir, this novelist and dramatist established his reputation with the ever-popular *Peter Pan*.

7 Hugh MacDiarmid (1892–1978)
A Drunk Man Looks at the Thistle is considered the finest poem by the "pioneer of the Scottish Renaissance".

8 Iain Banks (1954–)
Hugely popular author of *The Crow Road*, science fiction and psychological thrillers.

9 Irvine Welsh (1961–)
Best-selling cult author of street culture in Scotland. Made his mark in 1993 with *Trainspotting*.

10 J K Rowling (1965–)
This publishing phenomenon with global fame lived in Edinburgh when she launched the *Harry Potter* series.

Scotland's Top 10

Left **Antiseptic apparatus** Centre **Telephone prototype** Right **Dolly the Sheep**

🔟 Scottish Inventions

1 Rotative Steam Engine: James Watt (1736–1819)

While repairing a working model of a steam engine, Watt noticed deficiencies in its operation and hit upon a way to increase its efficiency threefold. His greatly improved engine had radical consequences for mechanical transport and industrialization.

2 Tar Road Surfacing: John McAdam (1756–1836)

Having made a fortune in New York, McAdam returned to his native Ayrshire in 1783 and began experimenting with crushed stones and tar. The endeavour cost him his fortune, but Parliament eventually remunerated him and made him Surveyor-General of Metropolitan Roads in 1825.

Light bulb

3 Bicycle: Kirkpatrick Macmillan (1813–78)

As a young blacksmith, Macmillan saw a child riding a hobby-horse and decided to make one of his own. He experimented with pedals and cranks, and in 1840 built the first bicycle, which he immediately rode from Dumfriesshire to Glasgow – a journey of two days.

4 Continuous Electric Light: Bowman Lindsay (1799–1862)

This prolific inventor devised an electric telegraph, recognized the potential for electric welding, proposed the first transatlantic submarine cable and demonstrated wireless telegraphy through water. However, he is best remembered as the man who gave us the light bulb, the first creation of continuous electric light.

5 Antiseptic: Joseph Lister (1827–1912)

The "father of antiseptic surgery" was working as house surgeon at the Edinburgh Royal Infirmary when he initiated the procedure of soaking instruments and surgical gauzes in carbolic acid. Results were miraculous, doing much to prevent fatal infections following operations.

Rotative steam engine

6 Telephone: Alexander Graham Bell (1888–1946)

Bell trained as a teacher of the deaf before being appointed Professor of Vocal Physiology in Boston, where he came up with the telephone prototype. "Yes, Alec, it is I, your father speaking" were some of the first telephonic words uttered.

7 Television: John Logie Baird (1888–1946)

Ill-health dogged Baird, but it also allowed him time to conduct research. Without financial support, he built a television apparatus from scrap materials and gave the first demonstration in 1926.

8 Penicillin: Alexander Fleming (1881–1955)

In 1928, a chance observation of a mould culture redirected Fleming's experimentation with antibiotics and led to his discovery of penicillin.

9 Radar: Sir Robert Watson-Watt (1892–1973)

Whilst working at the National Physical Laboratory, Watson-Watt developed a short-wave radio system that could locate aeroplanes. He called it "Radio Detection And Ranging". In 1940, he became scientific adviser to the Air Ministry, and radar quickly proved its value in World War II.

10 Dolly the Cloned Sheep: Roslin Institute (1997)

Cloning – producing an identical organism from a single cell of one "parent" – has been used to manipulate plant life for centuries. In 1997, scientists at Edinburgh's Roslin Institute produced the first successfully cloned mammal, Dolly, propagated from a single udder cell of a sheep.

And 10 More

1 Logarithm Tables
John Napier spent 20 years divising his ingenious system (1594) for multiplying and dividing large numbers.

2 Mackintosh
Charles Mackintosh gave his name to the rubberized waterproof material he developed in 1823.

3 Lawnmower
A "mechanical reaper" was how the Reverend Patrick Bell described the lawnmower he invented in 1826.

4 Fax Machine
Alexander Bain created the first machine capable of making facsimiles of original documents in 1843.

5 Anaesthetics in Midwifery
Sir James Young, the founder of modern gynaecology, first introduced ether, then chloroform as anaesthetics in midwifery in 1846.

6 Linoleum
This revolutionary floor covering was first produced by Frederick Walton in 1860.

7 Colour Photography
The physicist James C Maxwell produced the world's first photograph with three colours in 1861.

8 Pneumatic Tyre
Unprecedented comfort on rough roads was achieved in 1887, with John Dunlop's first air-filled tyre.

9 Thermos Flask
Designed for storing cold gasses, Sir James Dewar's vacuum flask (1892) soon came into everyday use.

10 Wave Energy
In 1973, Stephen Salter devised a system to generate electricity from sea waves.

Left **Celtic Connections** Centre **Military Tattoo** Right **Shetland fiddlers**

Cultural Events

1 Edinburgh International Festival, Fringe & Military Tattoo

The greatest extravaganza of music, drama, dance and opera on the planet. The Festival lays on the world's most prestigious performers, while the thousand-show Fringe brings the unknown and avante-garde. The massive spectacle of the castle's Military Tattoo is a swelling moment of national pride and vitality – a highly charged affair. ✪ *Festival: 11–31 Aug (approx); www.eif.uk • Fringe: 4–26 Aug (approx); www.edfringe.com • Tattoo: 2–24 Aug (approx); (0131) 225 1188; www.edintattoo.co.uk*

Jazz Festival

2 Glasgow Jazz Festival

A jamboree that swamps the city with devotees of jazz and supplies top international musicians. Venues range from theatres to pubs, clubs and ad hoc stages. ✪ *End of Jun and first week of Jul • www.jazzfest.co.uk*

Edinburgh Book Festival

3 Celtic Connections

The world's largest festival of Celtic music, with performers from as far afield as Mongolia and the Cape Verde Islands, as well as the Scots, Irish and Bretons. ✪ *Venues throughout Edinburgh • Mid-Jan–early Feb • (0141) 353 8000*

4 Edinburgh International Book Festival

Charlotte Square *(see p69)* plays host to this annual showcase of literary talent, bringing together the best-selling and most critically acclaimed authors for readings, debates and signing sessions. ✪ *9–25 Aug • (0131) 228 5444 • www.edbookfest.co.uk*

5 Edinburgh International Film Festival

Established in 1947, the festival now comprises four categories: world premieres, young British talent, film study and a major restrospective. ✪ *Filmhouse (Map L4), plus other venues • Mid- to late Aug • (0131) 229 2550 • www.edfilmfest.org.uk*

6 Edinburgh International Science Festival

Successfully combining education with entertainment in venues right across the city. The programme includes exhibitions of the latest scientific advances and demonstrations of tomorow's gadgets, as well as a platform for serious debate. ✪ *Early to mid-Apr • (0131) 220 1882 • www.scifest.demon.co.uk*

Science Festival

7 T in the Park

Sponsored by the brewery Tennents (hence the T), this is Scotland's biggest annual rock concert. The fields of Kinross are smothered in tents, while the bands get to perform in a giant castle of a marquee. ◈ Map F5 • Mid-Jul • www.tinthepark.com

8 St Magnus Festival

The beautiful Orkney islands have worked hard to create a festival of exceptional quality. Events usually include at least one world premiere of either music or drama, and some of the world's best musicians. Timed for midsummer, the festival uses Orkney's remarkable landscape to striking effect. ◈ Orkney • Late Jun • www.stmagnusfestival.com

9 Shetland Folk Festival

These islands are the heartland of Scottish fiddle-playing, and this festival not only showcases the prodigious home-grown talent but also attracts the best from far afield. ◈ Shetland • April • www.shetland-tourism.co.uk

10 Lanimer Day

Based on the annual custom of walking the town's boundaries (which started in 1140), this festival has developed into a week of fun events and fairground thrills. The highlight is the long parade of decorated floats, usually covered in thousands of paper flowers, and children dressed in outlandish costumes. A great community atmosphere prevails. ◈ Lanark • Early Jun • (01555) 661661

Top 10 Riotous Events

1 Hogmanay, Edinburgh
THE PARTY! Crowds pack Princes Street (ticket only) and the castle is lit up by fireworks (31 Dec).

2 World Pipe Band Championships
Astonishing sights and sounds as 3,000 pipers play on Glasgow Green (mid-Aug).

3 Glasgay
One of the UK's largest gay and lesbian festivals (1–14 Nov, Glasgow).

4 Royal Highland Show
Celebrating the biggest, best and most cultivated in the farming world (Jun, Edinburgh).

5 Edinburgh International Jazz & Blues Festival
A rival to Glasgow's, this is the capital's own festival of cool music (late Jul/early Aug).

6 Speyfest
The best folk and traditional music performers gather at Fochabers (between Elgin and Buckie, Map C5) in early Aug.

7 Up Helly Aa
An incredible fire festival. Men dress as Vikings and burn a replica longboat. (late Jan, Shetland).

8 Gig on the Green
All-day rock concert on Glasgow Green with a star-studded line up (mid/late-Aug).

9 Borders Rugby Sevens
Skill, passion and mud. In rugby's heartland, each border town takes a day as host (Apr/May).

10 The Ba', Kirkwall
Wild ball game and free-for-all played in the town's crowded streets (Kirkwall, Orkney, 1 Jan).

Left **Loch Skeen** Centre **Loch Lomond** Right **Loch Awe**

🔟 Lochs

1 Loch Trool
An enchanting loch within a forest, in a very much overlooked corner of Scotland, characterized by its stunning wilderness. The loch is bordered by walks, which form part of the long-distance Southern Upland Way *(see p42)*. At the eastern end there's a memorial to King Robert the Bruce. ◈ *Map H4*

2 Loch Skeen
The hidden treasure at the end of an utterly magical walk, Loch Skeen is a tiny loch high up in moorland hills. The walk to it climbs steeply alongside the spectacular Grey Mare's Tail waterfall (note that it's dangerous to leave the path en route). The visitor centre, situated near the falls, has a CCTV on a peregrine falcon nest. ◈ *Map G5*

3 Loch Lomond
The largest surface of fresh water in Scotland, Loch Lomond's beauty is celebrated in literature, song and legend. Now the country's first National Park, in conjunction with the Trossachs, the loch is revered for its islands, lofty hills and shoreside leisure facilities. ◈ *Map F4*

4 Loch Katrine
Famous as the inspiration for Sir Walter Scott's *Lady of the Lake*, this loch is the pearl of the area known as the Trossachs. Now incorporated into the National Park with Loch Lomond, it is sheer tranquillity compared with the other's bustle. The must-do here is to take a boat tour – the *SS Sir Walter Scott* (naturally) has been doing the job for over a century. ◈ *Map F4*

Loch Katrine

5 Loch Awe
A long sliver of a loch, twisting sinuously through forested hills. The magnificent ruins of Kilchurn Castle (begun 1440) stand at one end and testify to the stormy past of clan Campbell. Take the southern road for the best scenery, and don't be in a hurry. Close by is the defunct but preserved Bonawe Iron Foundry. ◈ *Map F3*

For all manner of useful information about lochs within the Trossachs and Cairngorms, check out www.JustOutstanding.co.uk

6 Loch Tummel

This small loch, with its shimmering brilliance, was a favourite of Queen Victoria, and you can stand at her preferred spot on the north side at Queen's View. The vista to the distant peak of Schiehallion is splendid, complemented in autumn by sweeps of colourful forest. Take the southern road to find the best picnic spots by the loch, and don't miss the river gorge walks at nearby Killiecrankie. ✎ *Map E4*

7 Loch Morar

The rival to Loch Ness, Loch Morar is Scotland's deepest loch (over 300 m/1,000 ft), and has long had its own legend of a monster – Morag (apparently identical to Nessie). Morar is easy to get to but little visited because its shores are largely inaccessible to cars, which makes it all the more delightful for walking. Nearby are spectacular beaches – the White Sands of Morar. ✎ *Map E3*

8 Loch Ness

Probably Scotland's most charismatic loch, this deep body of water is a major draw because of the scenic splendour of the Great Glen, Urquhart Castle and the as-yet-unexplained sightings of monster Nessie *(see pp24–5)*. ✎ *Map D4*

9 Loch Torridon

A magnificent sea loch that is reminiscent of a Norwegian fjord. The wall of red sandstone mountains to its north attracts hill walkers by the score, and from the summits you can see all the way from Cape Wrath to Ardnamurchan. A lovely one-way walk takes you from Diabeg to Inveralligin, with a series of

Loch Tummel

refreshing lochans (small lochs) in which to swim if the weather's hot. ✎ *Map D3*

10 Loch Maree

You'll pass this loch if you visit Inverewe Gardens *(see p51)*. Wonderfully situated among imposing mountains, Loch Maree is a revered fishing loch by a nature reserve. Red deer occasionally swim out to the group of wooded islands in the centre and make temporary homes there. ✎ *Map C3*

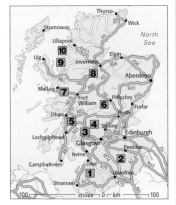

Left **The Five Sisters** Right **Buchaille Etive Mor**

Munroes

1 Ben Nevis
Britain's highest mountain at 1,343 m (4,410 ft). A long, winding path takes you up to the top. The summit is seldom clear of cloud, but if you strike it lucky you'll enjoy unsurpassed views. In poor visibility take great care on the summit ridge as it's easy to lose the path, which borders a precipice. ◈ *Map E3*

2 Ben Macdui
Britain's second-highest mountain, at 1,309 m (4,295 ft), is best climbed from the Cairngorm Ski car park. Reached by a high-altitude plateau covered in sub-arctic flora, it overlooks the magnificent Lairig Ghru, a deep rift dividing the Cairngorm range. ◈ *Map D5*

3 Ben Lomond
Rising proudly from the wooded banks of its namesake loch, Ben Lomond's tall mass dominates the panorama. One of

Definition of a Munro

Any Scottish summit over 3,000 ft (approx. 900 m) is called a "munro" after Sir Hugh Munro, who published a list of them in 1891. There are 284 munroes, and "munro-bagging" is a popular pastime. Most can be walked safely without climbing skills, but it is vital to plan well, be properly equipped and competent in map reading. Conditions can deteriorate rapidly at any time of year.

the smallest munroes at 973 m (3,192 ft), it has a well-used track, which is steep in places. Tremendous views over the Loch Lomond and Trossachs National Park. Best to start at Rowardennan, where there's a hotel and hostel. ◈ *Map F4*

4 Ben Vorlich
A great one to start with as there's nothing complicated about this hill, which overlooks Loch Earn, always bustling with boat activity. Take the southern road and start from Ardvorlich. From the top (985 m/3,232 ft) the views to the Breadalbane mountains are glorious. And it doesn't take long to get down for tea in St Fillans. ◈ *Map F4*

5 Ben Cruachan
A grouping, in fact, of seven peaks overlooking lochs Awe and Etive. The highest is 1,124m (3,688 ft)

Ben Nevis

and because this summit is considerably taller than any other mountain in the area, Ben Cruachan enjoys some of the most extensive views in the country. The name "Cruachan" comes from the war cry of the clan Campbell. ◊ Map E3

Liathach

The Five Sisters
6 A superb range of mountains with five prominent peaks towering above Glen Shiel in the West Highlands. If you start at the highest part of the main road (A87) you save yourself an hour's climbing. Once you're on the summit ridge it's a long series of undulations, but you feel on top of the world and can see the Cuillins on Skye. ◊ Map D3

Buchaille Etive Mor
7 The "Great Shepherd of Etive" (954 m/3,129 ft) stands as guardian at the eastern entrance to Glencoe. As an introduction to a place of legendary beauty, this wild mountain could not be improved. Approached from the southwest it can be climbed easily, but its magnificent crags demand constant respect. ◊ Map E3

Schiehallion
8 A much-loved mountain between lochs Tay and Rannoch, Schiehallion is most easily climbed from the pretty road connecting Aberfeldy with Tummel Bridge. An easy and rewarding munro with which to launch your bagging campaign. ◊ Map E4

Liathach
9 You could pick any of the famous Torridon mountains and guarantee not to be disappointed, but this is a beauty. A massive mound of red sandstone topped with white quartzite, Liathach has distinctive parallel bands of escarpments. At 1,053 m (3,456 ft) this is a relatively difficult and strenuous mountain to climb, but worth every bit of effort. ◊ Map D3

Ben Hope
10 The most northerly munro, with its neighbour, Foinaven. Rising starkly from the woods and moorland around Loch Hope, Ben Hope (927 m/ 3,040 ft) has clear views to the Orkneys. The only difficulty in climbing is the scree and rocky terrain, but this is a prestigious mountain to have underfoot. ◊ Map B4

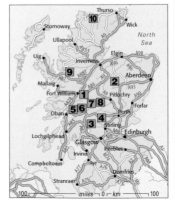

Left **Glencoe** Right **Dryburgh Abbey on the Border Abbeys Way**

📖 Walking Routes

1 Southern Upland Way

The longest walking route in Scotland, and a wonderful mix of mountain, moor, forest, loch and pasture. It crosses the country from Portpatrick in the west to Cockburnspath in the east – the preferred direction if you want the wind at your back. ⊗ Map H3–F6 • 212 miles (340 km) • 15–20 days

Speyside footpath sign

2 West Highland Way

The first long-distance route, and still the most popular. Connecting Fort William and Glasgow, it winds past the Nevis and Glencoe ranges, crosses Rannoch Moor and skirts around every other mountain it can find. Stunning scenery, but rather close to the main road in parts. ⊗ Map E3–F4 • 95 miles (150 km) • 7–10 days • www.west-highland-way.co.uk

3 Speyside Way

Bordering one of Scotland's most picturesque rivers, this path takes you from the Cairngorms to Moray's coast (with spurs to Dufftown and Tomintoul). It is a walk full of interest, with distilleries galore, bridges, stately homes and a rich abundance of wildlife. ⊗ Map D4–C5 • 66 miles (105 km) • 4–6 days

4 Great Glen Way

The newest route to open and the one that probably packs in more dramatic scenery per mile than any other. The walk connects Fort William with Inverness. The southern half offers easier gradients along the banks of lochs Lochy and Oich. After Fort Augustus it climbs high above Loch Ness – if that doesn't take your breath, the views will. ⊗ Map D4–E3 • 73 miles (117 km) • 4–7 days

5 Border Abbeys Way

A circular route that combines historical interest with the irresistible appeal of the gentle Borders landscape, with its rounded hills, rivers and forests. The track connects the four magnificent abbeys of Kelso, Melrose, Dryburgh and Jedburgh. ⊗ Map G5–6 • 65 miles (105 km) • 4–5 days

Landscape from Scott's View, near Melrose

The best maps for walkers are the widely available Ordnance Survey Landranger and Explorer series (www.ordsvy.gov.uk)

Fife Coast

6 Fife Coastal Path
One day this walk will connect the famous Tay and Forth Bridges. Currently it runs from North Queensferry, near Deep Sea World, to the East Neuk, taking in views across the Firth of Forth to Edinburgh, as well as the enchanting fishing villages of Earlsferry, Elie, Crail Pittenweem and Anstruther.
Ⓢ *Map F5 • 45 miles (72 km) • 3–4 days*
• *www.fifecoastalpath.com*

7 Cateran Trail
The Caterans, brigands and rustlers, roamed this area in the Middle Ages. Starting in Blairgowrie's soft-fruit hills, this circular route wends to the wild mountains of Glenshee, returning via beautiful Glenisla, offering some of the best of Perthshire. A quieter trail than most. Ⓢ *Map E5 • 60 miles (96 km)*
• *5 days • www.caterantrail.co.uk*

8 St Cuthbert's Way
The only cross-border route in Scotland. It starts in the abbey town of Melrose and ends on the amazing island of Lindisfarne (England). Not too strenuous a walk and a lovely mix of pasture, woodland, moor and coastal scenery. Check the tides for the last mile. Ⓢ *Map G5–6 • 62 miles (100 km) • 4 days*

9 Formantine and Buchan Way
An easy route for the simple reason that it's completely flat, running along an old railway line. It extends north from Dyce (Aberdeen airport) through the fertile rolling farmland of Buchan to the busy fishing port of Fraserburgh. Ⓢ *Map D6–C6 • 54 miles (86 km) • 4–5 days*

10 Cowal Way
If you like things a little wilder, try this one. The route is only partially marked, so take a good map. Start on the coast west of Glasgow at Portavadie and cross the hills to Glendaruel, Strachur and Arrochar. Ⓢ *Map F3 • 47 miles (75 km) • 6 days*

The Cateran Trail in Blairgowrie

Walking Routes
Aside from national long-distance routes, there is a vast network of local footpaths, and many areas have walking festivals. More details on all aspects of walking are available from these sites:
www.walkingwild.com
www.scotways.com
www.ramblers.org.uk/index.html
www.smc.org.uk

Berneray

TOP 10 Island Retreats

1 Gigha Hotel, Isle of Gigha

Even though it's only 7 miles (11 km) long by 2 miles (3 km) wide, the Vikings liked this island so much they stayed for 400 years. As well as tranquillity and sandy bays, the island is celebrated for Achamore House and its semi-tropical gar-den. ◈ Map G2–3 • (01583) 505254 • www.isle-of-gigha.co.uk • £

Breachacha Castle, Coll

2 Isle of Eriska Hotel

A tiny "Isle of Sanctuary", on which stands a superlative hotel: a baronial castle with as many down feathers and soothing fabrics as comfort could desire. A golf course, swimming pool, gymnasium, tennis courts and the freedom of the wildlife reserve are all at hand. Badgers turn up for milk at the bar most nights. ◈ Ledaig • Map E3 • (01631) 720371 • www.eriska-hotel.co.uk • £££££

3 Barnhill, Jura

George Orwell sought the isolation of this house when he came to Jura to write *Nineteen Eighty-Four*. You get to stoke the cooker with coal, much as the writer would have done in 1946. If you don't have a four-wheel drive you'll have to walk the last 5 miles (8 km). Check out the Corryvreckan whirlpool, but don't – as Orwell did – get caught in it. ◈ Map F2 • Bookings: (01786) 850274 • £

4 Camping in Breachacha Castle grounds on Coll

Loch Breachacha, and a corner of Utopia for £2 a night! Okay, you have to provide the canvas, but you get to live on a beach with views over the bay to Breachacha Castle. Simple facilities but this includes showers and you need no more on this wonderful island. ◈ Map E2 • (01879) 230374 • £

5 Port Mor House

Safe bathing, sandy beaches, colonies of puffins and wonderful isolation make the Isle of Muck (either isle of "pig" or "porpoises") a rat-race escapee's dream. Port Mor House is a well-established guesthouse, run by the family that still owns and farms the island. After a day's walking or beach-combing, indulge in superb and imaginative cooking. ◈ Map E2 • (01687) 462365 • £

6 Kinloch Castle Hostel, Rum

Share in the fantasy of this magnificent Victorian folly,

Price categories are calculated per night, but for self-catering cottages there is usually a minimum stay of one week

Kinloch Castle. Sleep in the castle bedrooms and dine at the bistro, or, for a cheaper option, stay in the former servants' quarters, a self-catering hostel. A great place from which to imbibe this beautiful and mountainous island. ◎ *Map D2 • (01687) 462037 • £*

Busta House Hotel

7 Eriskay
A self-catering flat close to the beach on a halcyon Hebridean island, now linked by causeway to South Uist. A rare convolvulus grows here, said to have been planted by Bonnie Prince Charlie to mark his first landfall in Scotland – Prince's Beach. Any stay is incomplete without a visit to Am Politician bar, with its relics from the ship in the British film classic *Whisky Galore*. ◎ *Map D1 • (01878) 720274 • £*

8 Berneray Youth Hostel
The Gatliff Hebridean Hostels Trust has restored two old blackhouses (cottages blackened inside by peat smoke) to make this hostel, overlooking the Sound of Harris. Berneray is Prince Charles's favourite island: its west coast is one long beach. Great walks and birdlife. ◎ *Map C1 • www.gatliff. org.uk • £*

9 Balfour Castle, Orkney
A castle with real home comfort, completed in 1848 to a slightly eccentric calendar design (it has 7 turrets, 12 entrance doors, 52 rooms and 365 panes of glass). This family-run hotel has style, class and great service. There are four-poster beds, open fires, a library and even a private chapel. A garden and locally-produced food with flavour add to the mix *(see p148)*. ◎ *Shapinsay, Orkney • Map A5 • (01856) 711282 • www.balfourcastle.co.uk • £££*

10 Busta House Hotel, Shetland
Britain's most northerly country house hotel is a 16th-century laird's home with a history that reads like a thriller. The whitewashed house combines character with elegance; winter visits are warmed by peat fires *(see also p147)*. ◎ *Brae • Map A1 • (01806) 522506 • www.bustahouse.com • ££££*

Barnhill, Jura, where George Orwell wrote *Nineteen Eighty-Four*

Left **Blair Castle** Centre **Balmoral** Right **Eilean Donan Castle**

Castles

1 Edinburgh Castle

The greatest castle in a land that's full of them, not only prized for its crowning position in the capital's heart, but also for its important history and the national treasures it holds *(see pp8–9)*.

2 Culzean Castle

Robert Adam's masterful design and exquisite taste reached their apotheosis in this castle, which ranks as one of Britain's finest mansions. Set in a park that does it ample justice, it commands a dramatic coastal position, looking seaward from the top of an Ayrshire cliff *(see pp28–9)*.

3 Caerlaverock Castle

A triangular ruin with immense towers, Caerlaverock still sits within a filled moat. Its history spans a siege by Edward I in 1300 and a luxurious upgrading shortly

Edinburgh Castle

Caerlaverock Castle

before its fall in 1640. Its yellow sandstone walls glow beautifully pink and orange in the afternoon light *(see p79)*.

4 Stirling Castle

Dramatically perched on crags overlooking the plains where some of Scotland's most decisive battles took place, this castle was one of the nation's greatest strongholds and a key player in her history. The gatehouse, Great Hall and the Renaissance Royal Palace are outstanding. Check out the programme for special events, from tapestry weaving to sword fights *(see p97)*.

5 Glamis Castle

This 17th-century fairytale castle is best known for its literary associations: Duncan's Hall provided the setting for the King's murder in Shakespeare's *Macbeth*. It also has a famous secret chamber and was the childhood home of the late Queen Mother. Rooms represent different periods of history and contain fine collections of armour, furnishings and tapestries. There's said to be a ghost about, too. The gardens were laid out by the great 18th-century landscape gardener "Capability" Brown.

Glamis Castle

🌐 Glamis, Angus • Map E5 • (01307)
840393 • www.glamis-castle.co.uk
• Apr–Oct: 10:30am–5:30pm • Adm

Blair Castle
6 Seat of the Duke of Atholl,
the only man in Britain still
allowed a private army, this
stately white castle is an
arresting sight on the main road
north. The oldest part dates from
1269, but after damage during
the Jacobite campaigns it was
completely restyled and all the
turrets added. 🌐 Map E4 • (01796)
481207 • Apr–Oct: 9:30am–5pm • Adm

Balmoral
7 This is the Queen's choice.
Queen Victoria purchased the
estate in 1852 and transformed
the existing castle into this un-
gainly but imposing mansion set
in spectacular grounds. It is still
the private holiday home of the
royal family, and provides a wonderful insight into contemporary
stately living (see p104).

Craigievar Castle
8 For sheer elegance, few
castles can match Craigievar. Its
cluster of towers held atop the
slender tower house (1626) is
a masterpiece of baronial
architecture and poise. The
interior retains the appearance
of the original Forbes family
home. 🌐 Alford, Aberdeenshire • Map
D5 • (01339) 883635 • Apr–Oct: 12–5pm
Thu–Mon • Adm

Cawdor Castle
9 Whether or not the real
Macbeth lived here in the 11th
century, it's the sort of make-
believe castle to satisfy all your
Shakespearean expectations.
Utterly magical with its original
keep (1454), a drawbridge,
ancient yew tree and enough
weapons to start an uprising.
The garden and estate are equally
enchanting and there's even a
maze (see p104–5).

Eilean Donan Castle
10 One of Scotland's most
photographed castles because
of its incredible setting –
huddled on an island off the
mountainous shores of Loch
Duich. This 13th-century
stronghold of the clan Macrae
was a ruin until its restoration in
the 1930s (see pp112–13).

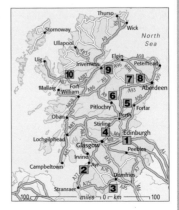

Left **Botanical Gardens, Glasgow** Centre **Arduaine** Right **Inverewe Gardens**

🔟 Gardens

1 Royal Botanic Garden

The capital's prize garden, with majestic trees, rock terraces, glasshouses and borders bursting with colour. A delight in every season. Watch out for the calendar of special events, such as music, theatre and exhibitions of contemporary art *(see also pp70–71).* ⑤ *20a Inverleith Row, Edinburgh • Map K5 • (0131) 552 7171 • www.rbge.org.uk • 9:30am–dusk daily • Free*

2 Dawyck Botanic Garden

An exciting outpost of the Edinburgh Botanic, where trees are the speciality. They began planting them here 300 years ago and have never stopped. The diversity is enormous and many specimens now rank as the finest examples of their kind. Ideal for great woodland walks in a particularly lovely part of the Borders. ⑤ *Stobo, nr Peebles • Map G5 • (01721) 760254 • Mar–Nov: 10am–6pm (Nov: 4pm) daily • Adm*

3 Kailzie Gardens

This formal walled garden is an outstanding example of what was once more common on family estates. Marvellous roses fill the air with fragrance, and there's a pond stocked with trout where you can try your luck at fishing. ⑤ *Kailzie, nr Peebles • Map G5 • (01721) 720007 • Apr–Oct: 11am–5:30pm daily; Nov–Mar: 11am–5pm daily • Adm*

Mercury, Kailzie Gardens

4 Logan Botanic Garden

The Logan boasts the greatest number of exotic species growing outdoors in Scotland. The southern hemisphere is particularly well represented and the palm trees and gunnera have grown to almost jungle proportions. Apart from the climate, there's a South Pacific feel to the place. It's usually much quieter than other gardens, too. ⑤ *Port Logan, south of Stranraer • Map H3 • (01776) 860231 • Mar–Oct: 10am–6pm daily • Adm*

Kailzie Gardens

5 Botanical Gardens, Glasgow

The city's magnificent gardens are especially noted for their glasshouses, packed with exotic plants. Foremost among these is the curved iron framework of the Kibble Palace. A wonderful oasis of palm trees, ferns, orchids and begonias is found inside *(see also*

Crarae Gardens

pp92–3). ✎ *730 Great Western Road, Glasgow • Map V1 • (0141) 334 2422 • Park: dawn–dusk daily; Glasshouses: 10am–4:45pm (4:15pm winter) daily • Free*

6 Crarae Gardens

A superb woodland garden with one of the country's most diverse collections of rhododendrons. Many of the seeds were originally gathered on private expeditions around the world and some species are now rare. In May the garden bursts into a brilliant mass of blooms and is worth travelling a long way to see *(see also p98).* ✎ *Nr Inveraray • Map F3 • (01564) 886614 • 9:30am–sunset daily • Adm*

7 Arduaine Gardens

Overlooking the sea, this garden has another famous rhododendron collection, but also includes exotic blue Tibetan poppies, giant Himalayan lilies and Chatham Island forget-me-nots. Painstakingly restored to glory by two brothers *(see also p98).* ✎ *Nr Oban • Map F3 • (01852) 200366 • 9:30am–sunset daily • Adm*

8 Inverewe Gardens

These world-famous gardens were nurtured into astonishing fertility in 1862 by Osgood Mackenzie, and became his life's work. Exotic plants, shrubs and trees from all over the world, in a stunning location on Loch Ewe *(see also p113).* ✎ *Nr Poolewe • Map C3 • (01445) 781200 • mid-Mar–Oct: 9am–9pm daily; Nov–mid-Mar: 9:30am–5pm daily • Adm*

9 Hydroponicum

A totally revolutionary place, the "garden of the future" has no soil but uses water to carry nutrients to the plants. Within this immense greenhouse they grow everything from tropical flowers to bananas *(see also p114).* ✎ *Achiltibuie • Map C3 • (01854) 622202 • www.thehydroponicum.com • Easter–Sep: 10am–6pm daily (last tour 5pm); Oct: 12:30–3:30pm Mon–Fri • Adm*

10 Pitmedden Garden

Originally laid out in a classical French style in 1675, this garden was re-created 50 years ago. Within a vast walled area are four elaborate floral parterres, three of them heraldic designs *(see also p103).* ✎ *Ellon • Map D6 • (01651) 842352 • Grounds: daily; Visitor centre: May–Sep: 10am–5pm daily • Adm*

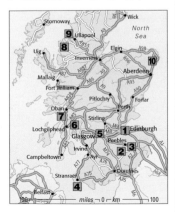

Left **The Tay** Centre **River Tweed** Right **River Findhorn**

Fishing Spots

1 River Tweed

The "Queen of salmon rivers" has the highest number of fly-catches of any British river. Autumn brings the greatest run, but purists say the quality of the smaller spring run is better. Beats are £30–£600 per rod per day. The Borders Tourist Office produce an excellent free guide *Fishing in the Scottish Borders*. ◎ *Map G5–5/F6 • 1 Feb–30 Nov • Borders Tourist Office: (0870) 6080404; www.visitscottishborders.com*

2 Loch Fitty

You can catch salmon here, but this well-stocked loch is best known for its trout (rainbow and brown). Fish from the bank or from a boat every day of the week during the season. There are B&Bs and a caravan park nearby, and The Halfway House Hotel – (01383) 731661 – is especially welcoming to anglers. ◎ *Nr Dunfermline • Map F5 • 15 Mar–6 Oct • Permits available locally • Contact: Fife Angling Centre (01383) 620666; www.lochfitty.com*

3 River Tay

The Tay is justly famed for its game fishing, and there's plenty of it in this long river. The cost varies greatly: in the Dunkeld area alone, for example, it can range from £20 to £150 a rod per day. Brown trout fishing can be as little as £3 per day in its marginally shorter season. ◎ *Map E4–5 • Salmon season: 15 Jan–15 Oct • Trout season: 15 Mar–6 Oct • Contact: Perthshire Tourist Board (01738) 450600*

4 River Findhorn

Some swear they'd never fish anywhere else. The Findhorn is a majestic river, flowing from the Monadhliath mountains through wild moorland, forest and farmland to one of the prettiest of all estuaries. As with all Scottish rivers, the fishing is weather-dependent, but in a good year its bag of salmon, grilse and sea trout can rank among the best. ◎ *Map D4–C5 • Permits available from The Fish & Tackle Shop at Forres (01309) 672936*

5 River Spey

Scotland's second longest river is its fastest flowing and can claim the most consistently beautiful scenery from end to end. Local village fishing associations offer relatively cheap day tickets, while private beats with the best

River Spey

reputations, such as Tulchan, command high prices. ✎ *Map D4–5/C5 • Feb–30 Sep • Grantown Association permits: (01479) 872684 • Tulchan Sporting Estates: (01807) 510200*

6 Sutherland's Rivers

Many of the fine fishing rivers in this area, such as the Shin, Oykel, Brora and Naver have occasional opportunities – easier for trout than salmon – for visiting fishermen (try Park House Sporting (01549) 402208) but are largely leased by syndicates. The River Helmsdale, however, has a first-class reputation and an association that offers day permits for salmon, sea and brown trout. ✎ *Map C4/B4–5 • Permits from Bridge Hotel Tackle Shop (01431) 821102.*

Assynt

7 Assynt Lochs

Superlative trout fishing in scenery to match. Walk into the hills with lunch and tackle, and find your own secluded loch from a choice of over fifty. ✎ *Map C3 • Fly-fishing only: 15 Mar– 6 Oct • Permits available at many outlets, including Lochinver Post Office (01571) 844330, Tourist Information Office (01571) 844262 and most local hotels*

8 Scrabster

With its tidal races, the Pentland Firth can be a wild stretch of water. It is a favoured haunt of fish such as cod, pollok, coal-fish, ling, mackerel and wrasse, all of which are regularly caught. The British records for halibut and portbeagle shark were set off Scrabster, but these species are rarely hooked now. ✎ *Map B5 • No closed*

Fishing, Helmsdale

season • Contact: Scottish Federation of Sea Anglers (01292) 264735

9 North Uist Lochs

With almost as much fresh water as land, North Uist is one of Scotland's hallowed trout fishing areas. Each season sees superb specimens caught from both bank and boat. Ghillies (guides-cum-gamekeepers) are available to show you the best spots and to advise on bait. ✎ *Map C1–D1 • North Uist Estate Office (01876) 500329; www.nuac.co.uk*

10 Orkney Lochs

Of the seven major lochs, Harray is the most renowned. Brownies (brown trout) are abundant, and there's every chance of a sea trout or even a salmon. Wading is recommended early in the season but a boat (which can be hired easily) is preferable in summer. ✎ *Map A5–B5 • 15 Mar–6 Oct • Contact: Orkney Tourist Board (01856) 872856; www.orkneytroutfishing.co.uk*

Left **Carnoustie** Right **Golf shop, Troon**

Golf Courses

1 St Andrews
Every golfer dreams of playing here. There are seven courses, including, most famous of all, the Old Course. Book months in advance or take your chance in the lottery for unreserved places held the day before. Fit in a visit to the Golf Museum too. The plush restaurant at the Old Course Hotel is listed on page 89. ✆ Map F5 • (01334) 466666 • www.standrews.org.uk

Golfer, Nairn

2 Carnoustie Championship Course
A delightful course, the superb links and great character of which have earned it a world-class reputation. You'll need to present your handicap certificate to play here (as at all the major courses) and reserve your tee in advance, but there are two other good links if you don't get on the main one. It's best to avoid the busy weekends throughout the year. ✆ Map E5 • (01241) 853789

3 Gleneagles
Another legendary group of courses, in beautiful moorland attached to a luxurious hotel. Queen's Course is the shortest, then comes King's and finally Monarch's, a marathon 6,475 m (7,081 yards). No handicap certificates required. Andrew Fairlie's delectable restaurant is listed on pages 65 & 89. ✆ Map F4 • (01764) 694469 • www.gleneagles.com

4 Gullane
Almost every blade of grass in this corner of East Lothian is dedicated to golf. Muirfield is the elite course but a private club. Gullane No. 1 is open to anyone (handicap certificate required), while Nos 2 and 3 have no restrictions. If Gullane's crowded then it's a short drive (by car) to North Berwick, Haddington or Aberlady, and seven more top courses. ✆ Map F5 • (01620) 842255 • www.gullanegolf.com

5 Glasgow Gailes
Despite its name, it's well down the coast from Glasgow and is considered one of the finest sea-edge courses. Great open vistas and fairways lined with heather add to its challenging holes. Western

St Andrews

For more about St Andrews, the "home of golf," see **p86**

Gailes runs alongside and shares all the qualities of its more famous neighbour. ❧ *Irvine • Map G4 • (0141) 942 2011 • www.glasgow gailes-golf.com*

6 Troon
Among the six courses here there's one for everyone, from Fullarton's fun course for beginners

Prestwick club house

to the classics such as Darley and Portland. But the best is the Old Course, a vintage Open venue. Apply well in advance (but no women allowed). ❧ *Map G4 • Old Course & Portland (01292) 311555; Darley, Fullarton, Kilmarnock, Lochgreen (01292) 312464*

7 Old Prestwick
New courses come and steal the limelight but Old Prestwick glows as an enduring favourite. In 1860 it was the very first venue for the British Open Championship, and it remains a beguiling and challenging course. One of Scotland's most venerated. Very busy, especially at weekends. ❧ *Map G4 • (01292) 477404*

8 Turnberry
Situated on the Ayrshire coast, the Ailsa Course has tested all the world's great players. A brand new course, the Arran, has just opened. Access is difficult unless you stay at the hotel. For expert tuition and a review of your game, contact the Colin Montgomerie Links Golf Academy, the multi-million-pound addition to the hotel. ❧ *Map G3 • (01655) 331000 • www.turnberry.co.uk*

9 Nairn
The two championship courses here boast the finest

greens in Scotland. The Nairn has a distinguished record of hosting major tournaments but also has a nine-hole course, the Newton, for holiday golfers. Nairn Dunbar is the other top-notch course. ❧ *Map D4 • Nairn (01667) 453208; Dunbar (01667) 452741*

10 Royal Dornoch
Ranked in the top ten courses in Britain, the Championship Course has 18 pristine holes. It was laid out by Tom Morris in 1877 and follows the natural contours of the dunes around Dornoch Bay. A wonderful setting and less pressurized than other quality links. ❧ *Map C4 • (01862) 810219 • www.royaldornoch.com*

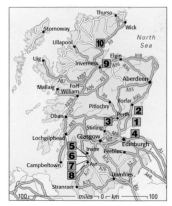

Left **Edradour** Right **Glenfarclas**

🔟 Whisky Distilleries

1 Laphroaig

With their heavy smoked-peat flavour, the Islay malts really are in a class of their own. Even if you think you won't like them, try them! This malt is pronounced "la-froyg", but in truth your pronunciation doesn't matter – the taste is famous enough for instant recognition. A delightfully informal and intimate tour with plenty of wit and grist at a fine sea-edge location. 🌐 *Nr Port Ellen, Islay • Map G2 • (01496) 302418 • www.laphroaig. com • Mon–Fri, tours at 10:15am and 2:15pm by appt only • Adm*

2 Lagavulin

Like its rival Laphroaig *(see above)*, this is a very distinctive malt. It is made in a traditional distillery with unusual pear-shaped stills. A highly personal tour without that feeling of mass-market hustle. 🌐 *Port Ellen,*

Glenlivet

Islay • Map G2 • (01496) 302400 • Mon–Fri, tours by appt only • Adm

3 Glenkinchie

A rare Lowland distillery, this one was founded in 1837 and is only 15 miles (24 km) from Edinburgh. This makes it a popular place to visit, and so rather crowded, but it's up to the task, with a state-of-the-art visitor centre.

🌐 *Pencaitland, nr Haddington • Map F5 • (01875) 342004 • Jun–Sep: 10am–5pm Mon–Sat, noon–4pm Sun; Oct–May: times and days vary • Adm*

4 Edradour

Established in 1825, this is Scotland's smallest distillery and its cluster of buildings has remained virtually unchanged for 150 years. To witness the process here is all the more delightful for its being in miniature. Only twelve casks a week are produced, making it (as they say) "a rare treat for a few". 🌐 *Nr Pitlochry • Map E5 • (01796) 472095 • www.edradour.com • Mar–Oct: 9:30am–5pm Mon–Sat, noon–5pm Sun; Nov–mid-Dec: 10am–4pm Mon–Sat • Adm*

5 Glenlivet

One of the first distilleries to come out of hiding and be legalized in 1824, the Glenlivet has been at the forefront of the

Glenkinchie stills

➔ *For an A–Z of information on Scotch whisky, check out* **www.scotchwhisky.net**

Speyside coopers at work

industry ever since. A fluent and comprehensive tour. The best bit is the musty warehouse where the whisky sleeps for 12–18 years. ✆ *Ballindalloch • Map D5 • (01542) 783220 • www.theglenlivet.com • Apr–Oct: 10am–4pm Mon–Sat, 12:30–4pm Sun • Free*

Glenfarclas
6 One of the few independent companies and justly proud of it. Established in 1836, this distillery is still owned and managed by the fifth generation of the Grant family. Tour the gleaming copper stills and then take a dram in the splendid Ships Room. ✆ *Ballindalloch • Map D5 • (01807) 500234 • www.glenfarclas.co.uk • 10am–4pm Mon–Fri (to 5pm Apr–Sep); Jun–Sep: 10am–5pm Sat • Adm*

Traditional whisky drinking vessel (quaich)

Macallan
7 Another of the famous Speyside brands, and one of the most modern visitor centres in the valley. Aside from a guided tour, you explore whisky-making using the latest interactive technology. For a modest sum you can become a connoisseur by prearranging an individually tutored nosing and tasting session. ✆ *Craigellachie • Map D5 • (01340) 872280 • www.themacallan.com • Easter–Oct: 9am–6pm Mon–Sat; Nov–Easter: 9am–5pm Mon–Fri • Adm*

Cardhu
8 The only distillery to have been pioneered by a woman and, aside from producing a distinguished single malt, it provides the heart of the Johnnie Walker blend. This is one of the smaller distilleries and charming for it. ✆ *Knockando • Map D5 • (01340) 872555 • Jul–Sep: 10am–5pm Mon–Sat, noon–5pm Sun; Oct–Jun: times and days vary • Adm*

Talisker
9 The only distillery on Skye and it's been producing a highly respected malt since 1830, legally at least *(see pp20–21)*. Tours last 40 minutes and are bright and informative. ✆ *Map D2*

Highland Park
10 Possibly not the most famous whisky (though definitely among the greats), but the best tour. Maybe because they're so remote, they try harder. Prepare to be taken through deep piles of malt drying in a delicious reek of peat. ✆ *Nr Kirkwall, Orkney • Map A5 • (01856) 874619 • www.highlandpark.co.uk • May–Sep: 10am–5pm Mon–Sat, noon–5pm Sun; Oct–Apr: times and days vary • Adm*

Left **Shinty** Right **Curling**

Highland Traditions

1 Kilts and Tartans
No one knows why Highlanders adopted this distinctive mode of dress or exactly when clans adopted a family "pattern" or tartan. The oldest tartan is dated at around AD 245, and by 1746 there were enough clan tartans to be prohibited for 38 years in a purge on Highland culture. Today, with over 2,000 registered designs, tartans are flourishing.

Kilt maker

2 Bagpipes
No sound is more evocative of Scotland than that of the bagpipes. The great highland pipes are played by pipe and drum bands, and by individuals playing for competition or dancing. Over

Young piper at Edinburgh Castle

the last two decades bagpipes have also emerged onto the stage of world music alongside every other conceivable instrument.

3 Highland Dancing
Vital ingredients of any Highland Games are the young, kilted dancers competing on stage. They leap and turn, endeavouring to execute the varied steps perfectly in time to pipe music. Among the most common are the Sword Dance, performed over crossed blades, and the Highland Fling. Look out, too, for demonstrations of the ancient tradition of step dancing, now being revived.

4 Gaelic Language
The rich language of the Gael can be seen on road signs and heard in shops in the Highlands and Islands. There are estimated to be 60,000 Gaelic-speakers in the country, their stronghold being the Western Isles, but even here it's a second language. Despite the increase in Gaelic-medium education and the success of Gaelic pop stars Runrig, young people appear less dedicated to the language and its use is in decline.

5 Highland Games
These are great summer spectacles that take place in communities across the land.

Most popular are the kilted strongmen in the "heavy events", which include hurling monstrous hammers and tossing the caber. This is a tree trunk that must be lifted vertically, carried at a trot and tossed so that it turns end over end. Packed with bagpipes, dancers and athletes, these games are an essential part of any visit.

Highland Games hammer thrower

focus on Gaelic song and music. Singers perform as soloists, duettists and as choirs, all aspiring to win the Mod's highest accolade, which is the Gold Medal. The instrument competitions are for bagpipes, clarsachs (small harps), fiddles, accordeons, melodions and keyboards.

6 Shinty
This sport makes football look dull. A sort of hockey without rules, this fast-moving game is terrific entertainment (it does have rules, but they're not apparent to the casual observer). Games take place during winter and spring in the Highlands, culminating in the Camanachd Cup Final, the nearest thing to a re-enactment of Culloden.

7 Curling
This sport – rather like bowls on ice – is the one in which the Scots usually excel at the Winter Olympics. Heavy circular granite stones are used, with a flat base and a handle on top. The curler slides the stone down the rink towards a bull's-eye and team mates, armed with brushes, polish the path ahead of the stone if more momentum is needed.

8 The Mod
This great music festival takes place in a different location each year and always attracts hundreds of top competitors. Conducted in formal dress and with a great sense of dignity, these competitions

9 Sabbatarianism
Commonly in the Western Isles, but also across many parts of the Highlands and Islands, Sunday is still strictly observed as a day of rest. Bed-and-breakfast operators may take in their signs, and loud music or washing hanging on lines may offend local sensibilities. Visitors may suffer inconvenience if they don't plan ahead.

10 Ceilidhs
Ceilidh ("cay-ly") is a Gaelic word for a visit among friends, but it has taken on the meaning of "a party". Sometimes it is just that, a hall with a band where everyone dances. At others it is a performance where people do a turn, singing, dancing or playing an instrument. They are great fun and even the smallest village hall may have world-class local or touring performers.

Dancers at a ceilidh

Left **M&D's Scotland's Theme Park** Right **Storybook Glen**

🔟 Attractions for Children

1 Our Dynamic Earth

Housed in a spiked tent, this electrifying exhibition is a great mix of education and entertainment. You travel through all sorts of environments, from volcanic eruptions to the Ice Ages. Stand on shaking floors and get caught in a real tropical downpour – lots of interactivity, powerful images and the full experience of television's *Walking With Dinosaurs* (see also p70). ◉ Holyrood Road • Map R3 • www.dynamicearth.co.uk • Apr–Oct: 10am–6pm daily; Nov–Mar: 10am–5pm Wed–Sun • Adm

2 Edinburgh Zoo

One of the world's great zoos, particularly noted for its marvellous penguin colony. Well over 1,000 animals can be seen here, including such fascinating and endangered species as red pandas, tigers, white rhinos, ring-tailed lemurs and poison-arrow frogs (see p71). ◉ Map J5

3 Deep Sea World

Simply the best aquarium to be found. Dazzling shoals and lots of dangerous water inhabitants. A conveyor-belt tour takes you effortlessly through this beautifully presented environment. A mesmeric experience (see p85). ◉ Map F5

4 M&D's Scotland's Theme Park

Huge fairground fun centre with everything that gravitational and centrifugal forces can do to you. Big wheel, free-fall machine, flying carpet, kamikaze whirlygigs and the giant "500 tons of twisted fun" roller-coaster. For the younger ages there are gentler water chutes and merry-go-rounds.
◉ Motherwell • Map F4 • (01698) 333999
• www.scotlandsthemepark.com
• Arcade: 10am–10:30pm daily; Rides: May–Aug: 11am–10pm daily; phone for times in Mar, Apr, Sep & Oct • Adm

5 Glasgow Science Centre

Housed in a landmark building, three entire floors of hands-on experiments, which puzzle, delight and demonstrate that science is miraculous. There's an IMAX screen with 3D films, too, and the world's first revolv-

Edinburgh Zoo

ing tower (see also pp18–19). ◉ Map F4

6 Kelburn Country Centre

The family estate of the Earls of Glasgow doubles as an adventure park. The surprise-packed Secret Forest gets the best vote, and kids go berserk on the Marine Assault Course and soft play area. Spectacular

Landmark Forest

displays of falconry and well-organized pony treks. ◉ Nr Largs
• Map F3 • (01475) 568685
• www.kelburncountrycentre.com
• Adventure Park: late Mar–late Oct: 10am–6pm daily; Secret Forest: late Mar–late Oct: noon–6pm; Grounds: all year • Adm

7 Aviemore Kart Centre

Children just seem to love noisy engines and burning their way round race tracks. For all budding Grand Prix champions, this is the place. There are courses and machines to suit all ages, and safety helmets are provided. The Bullit is the fastest kart. ◉ Aviemore • Map D4 • (01479) 810722 • www.aviemorekartraceway.co.uk • 10am–late daily • Adm

8 Landmark Forest Heritage Centre

A discovery and play centre on a tree theme. Join the squirrels on the Tree Top Trail, climb the tallest timber tower in the country or try sawing a log with a two-man cross-saw. There's also a Spider-man's delight of climbing apparatus. ◉ Carrbridge, nr Aviemore • Map D4 • (0800) 731 3446 • www.landmark-centre.co.uk • Apr–Aug: 10am–6pm daily; Sep–Mar: 10am–5pm daily • Adm

9 Storybook Glen

One for the younger visitors. A family theme park with giant-sized models of storybook characters for kids to crawl over and enter make-believe worlds. Nursery rhymes feature highly: Humpty-Dumpty, Pooh and Postman Pat are some of the happy characters present.
◉ Maryculter, nr Aberdeen • Map D6
• (01224) 732941 • Mar–Oct: 10am–6pm daily; Nov–Feb: 10am–4pm weather permitting • Adm

10 Beach Leisure Centre

Aberdeen has 10 swimming pools, but this is the one for flumes. There's a mini-flume for tots, but older children will be after the hairiest and scariest: the Pipeline, Wipeout and Tube. The last of these you negotiate on a tyre, while as for the other two … just close your eyes and hope for the best. ◉ Beach Promenade, Aberdeen • Map D6 • (01224) 647647 • daily (flume times vary) • Adm

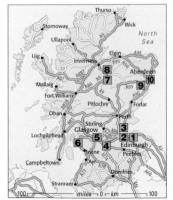

Left **Crovie** Right **St Kilda**

🔟 Best-Kept Secrets

1 Walk from Loch Morar to Tarbet

A combined walk and boat trip through sublime scenery. From Morar's silver sands, follow Britain's shortest river (half a mile) to the loch. Tarred at first, the way turns into an undulating track beside the water. It then wends to its destination at the lovely bay of Tarbet. Arrive by 3:30pm to catch the ferry back to Mallaig.
◎ *Map E3–D2 • 12 miles (20 km); approx 6 hours • Book the ferry (summer only) in advance: (01687) 462320*

2 Old Forge Music Venue

No juke boxes, video games, coach parties, briefcases or football colours. Instead, the Old Forge offers legendary music sessions, superb, unpretentious food, open fires and free moorings if you arrive by boat. The sea almost laps at the door, and Knoydart's scenery is equal to the best. Combine with the walk by Loch Morar. ◎ *Inverie • Map D3*

3 Sunset from Craig Youth Hostel

A simple, isolated cottage with five-star views over the sea to Skye and the Western Isles – sunsets are utterly breathtaking. Only accessible by foot, Craig is 3 miles (5 km) from Little Diabeg or 5 miles (9 km) from Red Point – and lovely miles they are too. You'll need to bring a sleeping bag, and bear in mind that there's no phone on site. ◎ *Map C3 • Scottish YHA (0870) 1553255; www.syha.org.uk • 10 May–31 Aug*

4 Foyers Falls

The more rain, the merrier for this one, so leave your visit until after a wet day – or seven! The upper falls are impressive; the lower falls even more so, plunging a spectacular 30 m (100 ft). The yellow-white torrent gushes into a black bowl, hollowed deep in the forest, and the almighty roar of the water is as inspiring as the magnificent sight. ◎ *Map D4*

5 Walk from Gardenstown to Crovie

It's only a short walk, about a mile (2 km), between these two captivating villages *(see p105)*, but don't let that deceive you. A few Tarzan-ish qualities are required, for in places your only links to Mother Earth are chains bolted to

Walkers' path by **Loch Morar**

Foyers Falls

the rock and toe-holds. Given these restrictions, it requires great care but is not hard. A mini-adventure amid rocks and grassy cliffs, ending in the secret world of Crovie. ◈ *Map C6*

6 Carbisdale Castle Youth Hostel

Could there be a hostel grander than this? Once home for the exiled King of Norway, the castle was built as a Romantic folly in 1914, with ballroom, library, marble fireplaces and a staircase of epic proportions. The art may not be the best but it looks the part, and sometimes there are more statues than guests.
◈ *Culrain • Map C4 • (01549) 421232*
• www.syha.org.uk • 1 Mar–26 Oct

7 Drive from Ullapool to Kylesku

Scotand's most beautiful road – drive it in spring when it's almost consumed by yellow-flowering whins, or in winter when surf erupts against the shore, or on a blue summer evening when Assynt's mountains assume the shape of absurd scribbles. But do drive it: take the A835 north from Ullapool, go west at Drum-runie, follow signs to Lochinver, then the B869 to Kylesku.
◈ *Map C3–B3*

8 Sandwood Bay

Perhaps it's the colourful strata patterning the rocks (Lewisian gneiss, among the world's oldest) or the quality of the sand. Perhaps it's the huge stack that stands sentinel at one end like some antediluvian shepherd. Or the Atlantic waves that charge in with billowing crests. Or is it the fact that so often you can have this mind-stretching expanse of beach to yourself?
◈ *Nr Kinlochbervie*
• Map B3

9 St Kilda

Scotland's first World Heritage Site, this archipelago of monumental cliffs was, until 1930, inhabited by a highly individual community who lived off the islands' millions of sea-birds. Such is St Kilda's isolation that it has its own subspecies of mouse, wren and sheep. Hard to get to, but if you can it'll touch your soul. ◈ *For info about visiting St Kilda, check out www.kilda.org.uk*

10 Regional Feis

A feis ("faysh") is a festival of Gaelic arts combined with work-shops. Lasting several days, most take place in the Highlands and Islands, always with terrific per-formances and blistering dances.
◈ *Feisean nan Gaidheal • Feb–Oct*
• (01463) 225559 • www.feisean.org.uk

Sandwood Bay

Left **The Witchery by the Castle, Edinburgh** Right **Three Chimneys, Skye**

🔟 Restaurants

1 Atrium

The Atrium garners its huge popularity from well-honed cooking, displayed in dishes such as a ragout of pigeon with foie gras, and roast halibut with a red pepper sauce *(see p77)*.

2 The Witchery

A wonderfully theatrical setting in the Secret Garden room. Game and seafood dominate the menu, while the 900-strong wine list carries a reputation of its own *(see p77)*.

Oysters on a bed of ice

3 The Tower

With access to one of the best views in Edinburgh, the food could easily take second place. But The Tower doesn't rest on its laurels, and continues to prepare simple Scottish dishes with carefully sourced ingredients – from oysters, mussels and scallops, to a hearty Aberdeen Angus steak *(see p77)*.

4 Amaryllis

Sophisticated cooking for a genteel dining room. Exquisite dishes – a succulent rare lamb fillet, perhaps, or mouthwatering scallops – are presented with artistry and a panoply of creative sauces. Worth every penny *(see p95)*.

5 Silver Darling

A long-established bistro run by Didier Dejean, perched so close to the mouth of the harbour you can almost touch the passing boats. Book upstairs for views to match a menu packed with sensational food. The bent here is towards chargrilling, and seafood is the speciality *(see p107)*.

6 Three Chimneys

You don't establish a restaurant in the remotest corner of Skye, win every award going and continue to run it to wild acclaim for 20 years without doing

The Tower

something right. Shirley and Bill Speirs do it perfectly in this old croft house, presenting local, fresh, simple, delicious food, cooked superbly. Make sure you book – an international trail leads here *(see p123)*.

7 Andrew Fairlie
Dine among Ionic pillars in a high-ceilinged room with blue-black walls and drapes of cream silk. The cuisine here is equally original, though the influence is markedly French. Try, for example, oak-smoked lobsters in lime sauce *(see p89)*.

8 The Peat Inn
Created a Chef Laureate in 1972, David Wilson's restaurant continues to enhance its reputation. Wooden beams, open fires and printed fabrics set a French provincial scene, which complements the style of cooking. Seasonal Scottish produce is to the fore *(see p89)*.

9 The Cellar
Tucked off a backstreet courtyard, everything about this fabled little bistro is unassuming, except, that is, the exuberance of the food. Apart from one meat dish (vegetarian dishes can be prepared by prior arrangement), the menu is entirely seafood, and chef Peter Jukes scours the local markets for the best of the day's catch *(see p89)*.

10 Airds Hotel
This fine country hotel has held a Michelin star since 1990. Seafood and game feature prominently but not exclusively, and Airds prides itself on the use of the freshest Highland foods, including Aberdeen Angus beef. They also do a wonderful poached-pear shortcake *(see p101)*.

Top 10 Scottish Dishes

1 Haggis
Scotland's most famous dish is like a large, round sausage containing spiced sheep's innards and seasoning. It's usually eaten with mashed "tatties" (potatoes) and "neeps" (turnips).

2 Venison
The meat of wild red deer, dark and full-flavoured. It's served as a steak or cut into collops (slices of roast meat).

3 Grouse
One of Scotland's prized game birds, this dark meat is roasted and served with home-made bread sauce.

4 Stovies
A mix of potatoes, onions and beef cooked in the dripping (fat) from the Sunday roast.

5 Kippers
Fresh herring split open, salted and smoked. A common breakfast dish.

6 Arbroath Smokies
Similar to kippers, but these are smoked haddock rather than herring.

7 Smoked Salmon
Thin boneless slices of salmon that have been smoked to give a rich taste and deep pink colour.

8 Scotch Broth
A light soup made from mutton or beef stock, pearl barley and various vegetables such as carrots and leeks.

9 Cock-a-leekie Soup
Chicken, leeks, rice and prunes cooked in chicken stock – as wonderful as its name.

10 Cullen Skink
Like chowder, this is a delicious soup made from smoked haddock, milk and mashed potato.

AROUND SCOTLAND

SCOTLAND'S TOP 10

Left **Castle guardsmen** Centre **Deacon Brodie's Tavern** Right **George Street in the New Town**

Edinburgh

WITH OVER 50 GOLF COURSES, 100 PARKS, *sufficient Neo-Classical architecture to dub it "the Athens of the North" and the crowning splendour of its castle, Edinburgh ranks as one of the world's most beautiful cities. Its centre is divided into two: the historic old town, with its cobblestones and narrow wynds (alleys); and the striking Georgian architecture of the New Town. Between them lies Princes Street Gardens, a bowl of greenery in the heart of the bustle. No other city crams in as many festivals during the year as Edinburgh, and in August it becomes the greatest showcase on earth for music, drama, dance and every other conceivable form of artistic culture.*

TOP 10 Sights

1. Edinburgh Castle and the Royal Mile
2. National Gallery of Scotland
3. Royal Museum and Museum of Scotland
4. New Town
5. Calton Hill
6. Our Dynamic Earth
7. Royal Yacht Britannia
8. Royal Botanic Garden
9. Scottish National Gallery of Modern Art
10. Edinburgh Zoo

Princes Street Gardens

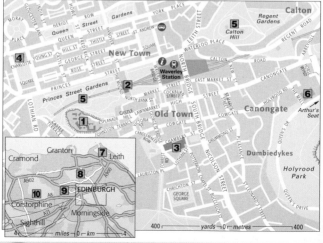

Previous pages **View over the city from Calton Hill**

Princes Street Gardens and the Castle, above

1 Edinburgh Castle and the Royal Mile

This world famous castle wears the nation's history. Here you'll find the Scottish Crown, Sword and Sceptre, and the legendary Stone of Destiny. The Royal Mile treads a straightish but diverting path from the Castle to Holyrood Palace (see pp8–11).

2 National Gallery of Scotland

Scotland's leading gallery includes masterpieces by the great Scottish artists, such as Raeburn and Ramsay, but is best known for its 15th- to 18th-century British and European paintings. In these collections, you'll find works by Botticelli, Velazquez, Raphael, Rembrandt, Rubens, Titian and many more besides (see pp12–13).

3 Royal Museum and Museum of Scotland

Two adjoining museums in radically different styles and with very diverse contents. Yet together they present the nation's most treasured historical artifacts. Worth visiting for the Lewis Chessmen alone, but don't expect to escape in under four hours (see pp14–15).

4 New Town

The New Town was the first daring adventure into planned architecture at a time of sordid living conditions for the masses. Begun in 1776, these beautifully proportioned buildings, set out in wide streets, crescents and squares, have lost none of their grandeur. The best place to start your walking tour is at the Georgian House, a restored mansion in Charlotte Square. Otherwise just wander wherever your eye is drawn. ◈ Georgian House, 7 Charlotte Square • Map L3 • (0131) 226 3318 • www.nts.org.uk • 20 Jan–24 Mar & 28 Oct–24 Dec: 11am–4pm daily; 25 Mar–27 Oct: 10am–6pm daily • Adm

Museum of Scotland

Left **View from Calton Hill** Right **Royal Yacht Britannia, Leith harbour**

Calton Hill
5 Rising above the town, Calton Hill is crowned by a gathering of Classical buildings: the Pantheon-like National Monument for the dead of the Napoleonic Wars, the Nelson Monument, commemorating the Battle of Trafalgar and the Old City Observatory. ⊗ *Map P2*

Our Dynamic Earth
6 Every bit as exciting and illuminating for adults as it is for kids, Our Dynamic Earth takes you on a journey through time from the Big Bang to the present. Amid this rapid evolution, environmental concerns are brought to the fore *(see also p60)*. ⊗ *Holyrood Rd • Map R3 • (0131) 550 7800 • www.dynamic earth.co.uk • Apr–Oct: 10am–6pm daily; Nov–Mar: 10am–5pm Wed–Sun • Adm*

Royal Yacht Britannia
7 From 1953 to 1997 this was the Queen's floating home, the honeymooning hotel of her

Princes Street Gardens

An area of neutrality between New Town and Old, these lovely gardens shelter under the wing of the clifftop castle. During the Festival they become a major events venue, and throughout summer the famous Floral Clock, comprising over 2,000 plants, ticks away in a corner by The Mound.

children and Britain's roving Royal court. Now you can wander the decks and cabins of this fabulous ship with an audio tour that tells of the life and times of *Britannia*. ⊗ *Ocean Terminal, Leith • Map K5 • (0131) 555 5566 • www.royalyachtbritannia.co.uk • Apr–Sep: 9:30am–4:30pm daily; Oct–Mar: 10am–3:30pm • Adm*

Royal Botanic Garden
8 Scotland's premier garden with trees, shrubs and flowers from around the world. Everything from hothouse palm trees and gigantic lilies to dwarf cacti and

Our Dynamic Earth

Scottish National Gallery of Modern Art

orchids. Look out for special events, and the guided tours will feed a curiosity you may never have realized you had (see also p50). ✆ 20a Inverleith Row • Map K5 • Free

9 Scottish National Gallery of Modern Art

This gallery only opened in 1960, but it has now amassed some 5,000 works post-1890. Here you can find the hand of such diverse figures as Picasso, Munch, Charles Rennie Mackintosh and the Pop-Art trio of Hamilton, Hockney and Tilson. Also check out the Dean Gallery opposite for contemporary shows (see p72). ✆ 75 Belford Rd • Map J3 • 10am–5pm Mon–Sat; noon–5pm Sun • Free

10 Edinburgh Zoo

You have to go to Antarctica to find a larger gathering of outdoor penguins. Here, in an underwater gallery, you can watch 150 cavort in the pool. The other highlights are the walkways over a re-creation of the African plains, where you can look down upon zebras, oryxes and ostriches (with a stunning, if rather mismatched, view of Edinburgh in the background), as well as marmosets and other miniature monkeys of the Magic Forest. But it's the penguins that steal the show. ✆ Murrayfield • Map J5 • (0131) 334 9171 • www.edinburghzoo. org.uk • Apr–Sep: 9am–6pm daily; Oct–Mar: 9am–4:30pm daily • Adm

A Day in Edinburgh

Morning

Have a leisurely start and be at the **National Gallery of Scotland** (see pp12–13) when it opens at 10am. Ninety minutes should allow you to see the Botticelli, Canova and Raeburn's skating minister, the Rev Robert Walker, as well as far more besides.

Enter **Princes Street Gardens** at the **Floral Clock** (opposite the gallery), and ascend the path to the **Castle** (see pp8–9), taking care as it's a steep climb.

Tour the castle, keeping an eye on your watch to make sure you're present when the **One O'Clock Gun** goes off – very dramatic! As you're now at the **Castle Café**, have a platter to restore your energy levels before soldiering on.

Afternoon

Stroll down from the Castle Esplanade to the **Royal Mile** (see pp10–11), stopping off at the **High Kirk** and probably several shops as well. Admire **John Knox's House** and have the best hot chocolate of your life in **Plaisir du Chocolat** on your left in the Canongate.

Turn right off the Royal Mile at Reid's Close (easy to miss) and visit **Our Dynamic Earth**, where you can pass several million years in the space of a mere two hours or so.

If you still feel energetic, walk up **Arthur's Seat** for spectacular evening views. Ninety minutes up and down (if you're fit) or grab a taxi and be chauffeured most of the way up.

Around Scotland – Edinburgh

Left **Open-top bus** Right **Wooden panel, Hopetoun House**

Best of the Rest

1 Open-Top Bus Tours
Cruise the city with guided commentary and a pigeon's eye view. ✆ Map N3 • MacTours: (0131) 220 0770 • Edinburgh Tour: (0131) 555 6363 • Guide Friday: (0131) 556 2244

2 Scottish National Portrait Gallery
Look Robert Burns, Bonnie Prince Charlie and the Queen Mother in the eye. Portraits through the ages, housed in a Gothic shrine. ✆ Queen St • Map N2 • www.nationalgalleries.org

3 Edinburgh Dungeon
Just when you thought you liked Edinburgh! The worst of the city's past: murder, torture, punishment, disease and grave robbing. ✆ Market St • Map N3 • (0131) 240 1000 • www.thedungeons.com

4 Greyfriars Kirk
Historic church, best known for its statue (in the street) of "Greyfriars Bobby" (1858–72), a devoted terrier who lived by his master's grave. ✆ Map N4

5 Dean Gallery
Opened in 1999, opposite the Scottish National Gallery of Modern Art (see p71), the gallery houses an art library and collection of works by Paolozzi. It also hosts temporary exhibitions. ✆ Belford Rd • Map J3 • Free

6 Hopetoun House
This fine architectural gem, work of the industrious Robert Adam, is both a stately home and an art treasury (paintings by Canaletto, Rubens, Rembrandt, to name but a few). ✆ Sth Queensferry • Map J5 • www.hopetounhouse.com

7 Caledonian Brewery
Intriguing tour of Edinburgh's famous brewery. Great copper vats and (smaller) samples. ✆ 42 Slateford Rd • Map K6 • (0131) 623 8066 • www.caledonian-brewery.co.uk

8 Edinburgh Butterfly and Insect World
A walk-through tropical forest with a myriad of free-flying butterflies and friendly crawlies. ✆ Lasswade • (0131) 663 4932 • www.edinburgh-butterfly-world.co.uk

9 Scottish Mining Museum
Don your headlamp and join ex-miners on an enlightening underground tour. ✆ Newtongrange • (0131) 663 7519 • www.scottishmining-museum.com

10 Crystal Visitor Centre
Amid blazing furnaces, watch molten glass turn into crystal – good place to pick up a bargain. ✆ Penicuik • (01968) 675128 • www.edinburgh-crystal.com

Left **Valvona & Crolla** Centre **Iain Mellis** Right **Hector Russell on Princes Street**

Places to Shop

1 Jenners
The oldest department store in the world, founded in the 1830s but occupying its present site since 1895. A miscellany of high quality goods and grand surrounds. ◈ *47 Princes St • Map N3*

2 Hector Russell
Made-to-measure kilts and a gathering of the tartans. Also a branch on the High Street.
◈ *Princes Street • Map M3*

3 Whistles
One of several boutique fashion stores that have made George Street their home over the last few years. High fashion for women. ◈ *97 George St • Map M2*

4 International Newsagent
The place to go to keep abreast of all the foreign news/ stories from back home. Good selection of foreign-language papers and magazines. ◈ *351 High Street • Map N3*

5 Iain Mellis
His cheeses are celebrated all around Scotland, and feature on many an Edinburgh menu, but the Victoria Street branch goes beyond matters dairy to embrace a panoply of culinary delicacies. Stock your hamper here.
◈ *30 Victoria Street • Map N4*

6 Halibut & Herring
Scottish handmade soaps and all manner of colourful, squeezy and curvaceous bathroom accessories in aquatic hues. A useful stop for pleasant-smelling presents. ◈ *Victoria St • Map N4*

7 West Port Books
One of a handful of independent bookshops just to the west of Grassmarket selling a mix of new and secondhand books. West Port's selection focuses on the arts. ◈ *West Port • Map M4*

8 Printmakers' Workshop
A range of limited edition works from contemporary print-makers at very reasonable prices. ◈ *23 Union Street • Map P1*

9 Valvona & Crolla
The best delicatessen in Edinburgh. Trading since the 1930s, Valvona & Crolla offer a wonderful selection of wines, great bread and fine Italian sauces. ◈ *19 Elm Row • Map P1*

10 Tiso
Before heading for the hills, check out Tiso for all your outdoor activity paraphernalia: boots, tents, climbing ropes and compasses galore. ◈ *41 Commercial St, Leith • Smaller branch on Rose St; Map M3*

Following pages **Loch Lomond**

73

Left **Café Royal Circle Bar** Centre **Bow Bar** Right **Deacon Brodie's**

Bars and Pubs

1 Bow Bar
Lush red and cream gloss paintwork envelops this modest room of a pub, where the sounds are provided by the jovial babble of conversation and clinking glasses. ✎ *Victoria St • Map N4*

2 Monboddo
Sharp-dressed slice of New York nightlife, set down amid the old-stone order of Edinburgh. Attached to the Point hotel *(see p143)*. ✎ *34 Bread St • Map L5*

3 Bennet's
Ever popular, its one-time ordinary pubness rapidly becoming exotic: big old mirrors, a mix of ages, drinks in pint pots and cheap lunches. ✎ *8 Leven St • Map L6*

4 Deacon Brodie's
Not especially remarkable by Edinburgh's high standards, but if you're on the Royal Mile (and you will be), it's a pleasant stop-off for a pint. Another ornate ceiling to peruse, too. ✎ *High St • Map N/P3*

5 Café Royal Circle Bar
Swirling ceilings, brass lamps and a convivial atmosphere of both young and old, at lunchtime enjoying simple seafood dishes from the kitchen of the Oyster Bar next door *(see opposite)*. ✎ *Map N2*

6 Dome Bar
A Corinthian-columned whale of a building, entered through a flight of steps flanked by nocturnal doormen. Ballooning chandeliers,
palm plants and a choice of bars: the vast and theatrical circle bar or the plush and cushioned side bar, with its evocation of the 1930s. ✎ *George St • Map M2*

7 Opal Lounge
Popular, chic dj bar, with a cosy backroom dining space. The low-lit rooms provide plenty of space for chatting, as well as shaking a leg. ✎ *George St • Map M2*

8 Rick's Bar
Bar, restaurant and rooms, in fact *(see p143)*. Sleek design warmed by rich, earthy hues and quiet mood lighting. ✎ *55a Frederick St • Map M2*

9 Indigo Yard
More intent on creating a vibe than simply serving drinks and food, Indigo Yard is good for lazy afternoons and carousing evenings. ✎ *7 Charlotte La • Map K3*

10 The Cumberland
Much-loved pub, its lights beckoning on cold winter nights, its pleasant side garden equally coquettish in the summer heat. ✎ *Cumberland St • Map M1*

Price Categories

For a three-course
meal for one with half
a bottle of wine (or
equivalent meal), taxes
and extra charges.

£	under £15
££	£15–£25
£££	£25–£35
££££	£35–£50
£££££	over £50

Left **The Witchery by the Castle** Right **The Tower**

🔟 Places to Eat

1 The Atrium
Unassuming side room off the Traverse foyer, serving some of the best food (Modern European) in Edinburgh. ◈ *10 Cambridge St • Map L4 • (0131) 228 8882 • £££££*

2 The Witchery by the Castle
Aim for the Secret Garden room to experience the Witchery at its romantic best. Excels at dishes with a rural flavour: honey-roasted duck, terrines of venison and pheasant. ◈ *Castlehill • Map M4 • (0131) 225 5613 • £££££*

3 The Dial
Sharp subterranean restaurant, plying Scottish produce mixed with international flair. Good for vegetarians, too – even haggis can be meatless! ◈ *44–46 George IV Bridge • Map N4 • (0131) 225 7179 • £££*

4 The Tower
Great location, eyeing up the Castle from the Museum of Scotland's rooftop. Tasty variations on Scottish cuisine. ◈ *Chambers St • Map N4 • (0131) 225 3003 • ££££*

5 Howie's
Local chain, recognizable by the cream-and-blue seaside paintwork. European-based menu; excellent value. ◈ *Victoria St • Map N4 • (0131) 225 1721 • ££*

6 Olorosso
Elevated in attitude and altitude, this rooftop glass box offers views, well-mixed cocktails and a menu that emphasizes precision over showmanship. ◈ *33 North Castle St • Map L3 • (0131) 226 7614 • ££££*

7 Le Café St-Honoré
Bistro food that's both familiar and better than ever – the result of scouring the markets at dawn. A charmer! ◈ *34 North West Thistle St La • Map M2 • (0131) 226 2211 • £££*

8 Café Royal Oyster Bar
Seafood classics – oysters on ice, soups and delicately cooked fillets. All amid Victorian splendour. ◈ *17a West Register St • Map N2 • (0131) 556 4124 • ££££*

9 A Room in the Town
Friendly bistro, where international trade results in haggis with smoked cheddar and Serano ham, and terrines of Ayrshire bacon and seared scallops. BYOB. ◈ *18 Howe St • Map L2 • (0131) 225 8204 • £*

10 Fishers, Leith
Love, as much as praise, has been heaped on this waterfront seafood restaurant, and for good reason: the cooking is honed; the ambience warm. ◈ *1 The Shore, Leith • (0131) 554 5666 • £££ • Sister restaurant, Fishers in the City, is at 58 Thistle St (M2)*

Left **Burns Museum** Right **Culzean Castle**

Southern Uplands

A BEAUTIFUL REGION OF ABRUPT AND ROLLING HILLS, *sheep pastures, forested valleys and soporific rivers, Southern Scotland is the home of rugby, Robert Burns, Sir Walter Scott and spectacular castles and abbeys. For centuries this border country was the flashpoint of hostility between Scotland and England, but also a centre of commerce and religion. The monuments of these times represent some of the best medieval and Renaissance architecture in Europe. Still sparsely inhabited, the border towns contest their rugby reputations in winter and, with equal passion, celebrate ancient riding festivals in summer.*

Melrose Abbey

🔟 Sights

1. Culzean Castle
2. New Lanark
3. Drumlanrig Castle
4. Caerlaverock Castle
5. The Falkirk Wheel
6. Linlithgow Palace
7. Rosslyn Chapel
8. Melrose Abbey
9. Dryburgh Abbey
10. Mellerstain House

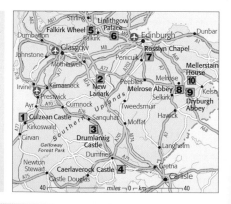

New Lanark

Caerlaverock Castle

In a land of ruined castles, this massive triangle of crafted stone, still standing within a filled moat, is exceptional. Its towers and walls are remarkably complete, despite having lain in ruin for 400 years *(see also p46)*. ◈ *Nr Dumfries • Map H5 • (01387) 770244 • Apr–Sep: 9:30am–6:30pm daily; Oct–Mar: 9:30am–4:30pm Mon–Fri, 2–4pm Sun • Adm*

Culzean Castle

This cliff-edge castle was re-modelled into a magnificent home for the Earls of Cassillis in 1777 by Georgian architectural master Robert Adam *(see pp28–9)*.

New Lanark

In 1820, at the height of the Industrial Revolution, factory owner Robert Owen recognized the need for safe and efficient working conditions, matched by good quality housing for his workers. New Lanark was the result, a modern industrial town that also boasted an education system (including the world's first nursery school) and free healthcare. Now a UNESCO World Heritage Site, this living museum still looks pioneering today. ◈ *Map G4 • 11am–5pm daily • Adm*

Drumlanrig Castle

Towering above its splendid woods, this castle of turrets and spiked domes is home to the Duke of Buccleuch. Begun in 1676, it was such a lavish undertaking that it almost ruined the family, but they bounced back and filled it with treasures. Particularly enticing are the silverware and rich oak panelling. Great walks and cycleways in the vicinity. ◈ *Map G4 • May–mid-Sep: 11am–4pm daily (Sun from noon) • Closed 2 weeks in mid-Aug*

The Falkirk Wheel

Resembling a science-fiction film set, this engineering marvel is a "world's first". In order to connect two canal systems on different levels, engineers came up with the idea of using revolving scoops. Canal boats enter what is essentially a giant bucket containing 300,000 gallons of water. Gates close, the wheel revolves and boats are carried up or down to the next level. Ingenious and fascinating to watch in motion. Visitors can ride the wheel in special boats. ◈ *Map F4 • (08700) 500208 • www.thefalkirk-wheel.co.uk • Boat trips: 9am–5pm daily; adm • Visitor Centre: 9am–6pm daily; free*

Caerlaverock Castle

For walking routes in the Southern Uplands see p42

Rosslyn Chapel

Linlithgow Palace

6 One of only four royal palaces in Scotland, Linlithgow was the birthplace of Mary Queen of Scots and provided a temporary safe haven for Bonnie Prince Charlie during the Jacobite Rebellion *(see pp32–3)*. Solid and fortress-like on the banks of Loch Linlithgow, the palace still looks majestic in its semi-ruined state. This was the finest building of its day, and its master masons have left a wealth of carvings. Look around the Great Hall and chapel and marvel at the expertise of the craftsmen who laboured upon this wonderful building. *Linlithgow • Map F5 • (01506) 842896 • Apr–Sep: 9:30am–6:30pm daily; Oct–Mar: 9:30am–4:30pm Mon–Sat, 2–4:30pm Sun • Adm*

Rosslyn Chapel

7 As extraordinary as it is mysterious. You'd be hard pushed to cram more carvings into such a small place – and what carvings! Built in 1446, it seems that every master mason had to do a turn here, such is the variety of styles and subjects. Most curious of all are the carvings of New World plants. They predate Columbus's transatlantic voyage of discovery by one hundred years – experts are dumbfounded, but the results speak for themselves. *Rosslyn • Map F5 • www.rosslyn-chapel.com • 10am–5pm Mon–Sat; from noon Sun • Adm*

Melrose Abbey

8 The tall lancet windows of this immensely impressive ruin must have appeared miraculous to medieval worshippers. And today, it's hard to believe that such monuments could have been built as early as 1136. Over the centuries, the abbey succumbed to pillage and war damage, and now stands as a beleaguered but romantic spot for the ghost of Robert the Bruce *(see pp96–7)*, whose heart is believed to reside within these grounds. *Melrose • Map G5 • Apr–Sep: 9:30am–6:30pm daily; Oct–Mar: 9:30am–4:30pm Mon–Sat, 2–4:30pm Sun • Adm*

Dryburgh Abbey

Mellerstain House

9 Dryburgh Abbey

Located on a bend in the River Tweed, these are the most beautiful and evocative ruins in Southern Scotland. Founded in 1152, the abbey was destroyed by the English in 1322, 1344 and again in 1385, but each time it rose to magnificence once more, until it was finally consumed by fire in 1544. Despite having lain in ruin for 500 years, it is remarkably complete, and the quality of masonry is unbelievable. See it when shadows fall for the most spectacular views. ◈ Nr St Boswells • Map G6 • (01835) 822381 • www.historic-scotland.net • Apr–Sep: 9:30am–6:30pm daily; Oct–Mar: 9:30am–4:30pm Mon–Sat, 2–4:30pm Sun • Adm

10 Mellerstain House

Scotland's most splendid Georgian house (early 18th century) is another creation by the famous architect Robert Adam. A vast edifice of perfect symmetry on the outside contains rooms of perfect proportions within. The delicate plasterwork of the library, resembling fine china in its precision, is considered one of Adam's greatest accomplishments. Exquisite details abound throughout the interior, while, outside, splendid terraced gardens run down to an ornamental lake. ◈ Gordon • Map G6 • Easter & May–Sep: 12:30–5pm Wed–Mon; Oct: Sat & Sun • Adm

Tour of the Abbeys

Morning

🕐 If you want to be flexible about where and when to eat, then shop at **Valvona & Crolla** or **Iain Mellis** (for both see p73) the day before your trip, and make a gourmet picnic – as lavish as you like.

The next morning, set off at 9am, just after rushhour, and drive to **Rosslyn Chapel** to see the extra-ordinary carvings. As wonderful as they are, this stop won't take long. So, before being tempted to delve into the hamper, drive on to Penicuik and take the A703 to **Peebles**. It's worth having a break for coffee in this pretty town.

Now take the lovely Tweedside A72 to **Melrose**. Visit the majestic abbey and then either lunch here at Marmions or drive on 5 miles (8 km) to **Scott's View** – one of the best in the Borders – and have your picnic at last.

Afternoon

If you haven't overdosed on the remnants of medieval monastic life, then make a brief visit to **Dryburgh Abbey**, the ruins and situation of which are very different to Melrose.

From Dryburgh it's a short drive to Earlston to visit nearby **Mellerstain House**. Start with a cup of tea and a sugary energy boost in the restaurant, and then tour at your leisure (it closes at 5pm in summer). Leave your stroll around the gardens till last as they close later.

Return to Edinburgh, or tour further along this border landscape.

Left **Abbotsford House** Right **Burns' Cottage**

Best of the Rest

1 Scottish Seabird Centre

Remote cameras relay live action from the Bass Rock's 100,000 gannets. Take time for a boat trip around the headland too. *North Berwick • Map F5 • (01620) 890202 • www.seabird.org • Summer: 10am–6pm daily; winter: 10am–4pm Mon–Fri, 10am–5:30pm Sat & Sun • Adm*

2 Abbotsford House

Wonderfully eccentric collection of weaponry and historical bric-a-brac, collected by the great novelist Sir Walter Scott and displayed in his dream home. *Nr Melrose • Map G6 • (01896) 752043 • 17 Mar–1 Nov: 9:30am–5pm Mon–Sat, 2–5pm Sun (Jun–Sep: 9:30am–5pm Sun) • Adm*

3 Traquair House

A romantic chateau, this is Scotland's oldest continually inhabited house (900 years) and a former pleasure ground for kings. *Innerleithen, nr Peebles • Map G5 • (01896) 830323 • 12 Apr–31 Oct: noon–5pm daily • Adm*

4 Burns National Heritage Park

Comprising a museum and the writer's cottage, this place of pilgrimage celebrates the life and genius of Scotland's national poet. *Alloway, nr Ayr • Map G4 • (01292) 443700 • www.robertburns.org*

5 Manderston House

The swansong of the great classical house, this family home stands in sumptuous gardens and has the only silver staircase in the world. *Duns • Map F6 • (01361) 883450 • www.manderston.co.uk.*

6 Scott's View

Sir Walter Scott's favourite view of the River Tweed and Eildon Hills. Out of habit, his horse stopped here during Scott's funeral procession. *Nr Dryburgh Abbey on the B6356 road • Map G6*

7 Galloway Forest Park

Area of superb loch, forest and hill scenery. Take a picnic to the Bruce's Stone or have a day out on foot or on bikes. *Map H4*

8 St Abb's Head

A national nature reserve on dramatic cliffs packed with birds. Don't miss the characterful town of St Abbs, with its excellent fishery museum. *Map F6*

9 Wigtown

Pretty seaside town that has become Scotland's "book town", full of all sorts of literary specialities and events. The Box of Frogs bookshop is heaven for children. *Wigtown • Map H4 • www.wigtown-booktown.co.uk*

10 Creetown Gemrock Museum

A thrilling collection of precious stones, crystals, minerals and fossils in a gem of a village on this sleepy coastline. *Wigtown Bay • Map H4 • (01671) 820357 • www.gemrock.net • Easter–Sep: 9:30am–5:30pm daily; winter: 10am–4pm daily, except Dec–Feb (weekends only) • Adm*

Price Categories

For a three-course meal for one with half a bottle of wine (or equivalent meal), taxes and extra charges.

£	under £15
££	£15–£25
£££	£25–£35
££££	£35–£50
£££££	over £50

Philipburn Country House

🔝10 Places to Eat

1 Fouters
Since the 1980s the Blacks have been dedicated to creating marvels with the best of local ingredients. Excellent, informal bistro. 🌑 *2a Academy St, Ayr • Map G4 • (01292) 261391 • Closed Sun • £££*

2 Knockinaam Lodge
Traditional food with a modern touch in a sumptuous country house. Memorable seafood, such as a simple dish of pan-seared scallops. Order vegetarian meals in advance. 🌑 *Portpatrick • Map H3 • (01776) 810471 • ££££*

3 Philipburn Country House
Bistro and restaurant offering light snacks to full meals. It maintains a country-house atmosphere, yet is very good value. Non-smoking. 🌑 *Selkirk • Map G5 • (01750) 720747 • £££*

4 Plumed Horse
A new discovery in an unexpected place. Seriously high quality modern cuisine prepared by chef Tony Borthwick. Gaining popularity by the day, so advance booking is advised.
🌑 *Crossmichael, nr Castle Douglas • Map H4 • (01556) 670333 • Closed: Sat & Mon lunch; Sun & Mon dinner • ££££*

5 The Crook Inn
Ancient den of hospitality offering simple wholesome food. Fillet steak topped with haggis inside a pastry case is one of the restaurant's wilder adventures. 🌑 *Tweedsmuir • Map G5 • (01899) 880272 • £*

6 Nardini's
Nardini's is a Scottish landmark – a bright cavern of ice cream, chips and chocolate, plus an array of Italian dishes. 🌑 *Largs • Map F3 • (01475) 674555 • £*

7 Marmions
Long-running French-feel brasserie, popular with locals and visitors. Snacks, full and rich à la carte and wines for all tastes.
🌑 *Buccleuch St, Melrose • Map G5 • (01896) 822245 • Closed Sun • £££*

8 Churches
Modern classy dining room with conservatory and outside tables in summer. Everything from light snacks to haute cuisine. 🌑 *Albert Rd, Eyemouth • Map F6 • (01890) 750401 • ££££*

9 Tibbie Shiels Inn
"Olde worlde" atmosphere and a bold menu of unpretentious food with four different vegetarian dishes daily. 🌑 *St Mary's Loch, Selkirk • Map G5 • (01750) 42231• ££*

10 The Auld Alliance
French-Scottish cuisine, well priced, and the Solway scallops come highly recommended.
🌑 *5 Castle Street, Kirkcudbright • Map H4 • (01557) 330569 • Open Easter–Oct • £££*

Marmions Brasserie

> **Note:** Unless otherwise stated, all restaurants accept credit cards and serve vegetarian meals

Left **Falkland Palace** Right **East Neuk**

North and East of Edinburgh

A TWO-HOUR DRIVE FROM EDINBURGH *takes you into the majestic Highland-like landscape of Perthshire or the rich farmland of Fife, with its coastal fringe of pretty villages. This is Scotland at its most diverse, with famous castles, abbeys, ships, bridges, wildlife reserves and golf courses all found within easy reach of each other by car. Scotland's greatest sporting tradition, golf, is much in evidence – especially in St Andrews, the sport's spiritual home – while the many castles and palaces testify to the enduring appeal of this pleasurable region.*

🔟 Sights

1 Deep Sea World
2 Culross
3 Dunfermline Abbey and Palace
4 East Neuk
5 St Andrews
6 Falkland Palace
7 Perth
8 Discovery Point
9 Glamis Castle
10 Pitlochry

Memorial Arch, Killiecrankie

East Neuk, Pittenweem harbour

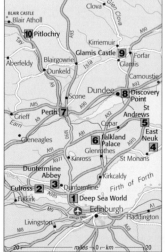

Dunfermline Abbey

1 Deep Sea World

Innovative presentation has made this aquarium a phenomenal success. Not only does it seem to have every imaginable species of dangerous, beautiful and ugly fish, but it also houses them in a network of glass tunnels, so that great shoals of glittering fish surround you. The more adventurous can even swim with sharks! ✎ *North Queensferry • Map F5 • (0906) 9410077 • www.deepseaworld.com • Apr–Oct: 10am–6pm daily; Nov–Mar: 11am–5pm Mon–Fri, 10am–6pm Sat & Sun • Adm*

2 Culross

Once a thriving village with mines, iron workings and trade links with the Low Countries, Culross fell into decline in the 18th and 19th centuries and became a forgotten backwater. Its restoration began in the 1930s, and now the town is a striking resurrection of its 16th- and 17th-century heyday. Even the plants in the palace garden are in keeping with the 1600s! ✎ *Map F5 • Palace: (01383) 880359 • www.nts.org.uk • 25 Mar–28 Jun, 2 Sep–27 Oct: noon–5pm daily; 29 Jun–1 Sep: 10am–6pm daily • Adm*

3 Dunfermline Abbey and Palace

Founded in the 11th century by Queen (later St) Margaret *(see p8)*, the abbey's stunning feature is the 12th-century Romanesque nave. This was the burial place of Robert the Bruce – without his heart, which he requested be taken on a crusade to the Holy Land. A skeleton with the heart chamber cut open was discovered in a grave here in 1818; the site is now marked by a plaque to honour the hero of Bannockburn *(see p32)*. ✎ *Dunfermline • Map F5 • (01383) 739026 • www.historic-scotland.net • Apr–Sep: 9:30am–6:30pm daily; Oct–Mar: 9:30am–4:30pm Mon–Sat, 2pm–4:30pm Sun • Closed Fri & Sun am, Thu pm • Adm*

4 East Neuk

"Neuk" is a Scots word for corner, and the East Neuk refers to a small bend in the coastline along which are found a remarkable chain of picturesque fishing villages. They run from Earlsferry to Crail, and every one is a gem. Elie and Crail are probably the most quaint and are favoured haunts of artists. Pittenweem's beautiful harbour is a still working port, and Anstruther, a haven for yachts, has a bustling seafront, where it's impossible not to buy ice cream. Its Scottish Fisheries Museum *(see p88)* is excellent. ✎ *Map F5–6*

Culross

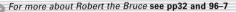

For more about Robert the Bruce see pp32 and 96–7

St Andrews

5 St Andrews

The "home of golf" *(see pp54–5)* has the oldest university in Scotland, and red-robed students add a colourful, carefree atmosphere to this pretty town. Once the ecclesiastical capital of the country, its cathedral is still a proud ruin, with a wealth of sculpture, and its castle has unrivalled examples of siege tunnels and a curious "bottle dungeon". There's also a mile of beach for fine walks, and plenty of hip cafés and bistros. ֍ *Map F5 • Cathedral & Castle both open Apr–Sep: 9:30am–6:30pm daily; Oct–Mar: 9:30am–4:30pm daily • Adm*

6 Falkland Palace

A wonderful sense of history pervades this palace, the home of Mary Queen of Scots and the Stuart kings from 1541. Restored royal bedchambers and fine 17th-century tapestries are on display, but most intriguing of all is the oldest real tennis court still in use in Britain, built in 1539. Unlike the modern game, real tennis was played indoors and shares some similarities with squash. ֍ *Map F5 • (01337) 857397 • www.nts.org.uk • 1 Mar–27 Oct: 10am–6pm Mon–Sat, 1pm–5pm Sun • Adm*

7 Perth

The "Fair City", as it is known, is attractively situated on the tree-lined River Tay. Despite a complicated one-way system, its streets are a delight of small-time shops, and it is one of Scotland's prime spots for browsing and buying. Though it does not boast any notable historical buildings itself, Perth makes a great centre for touring many others found within a short drive. A lovely walk takes you up to a folly on Kinnoull Hill and from here the views are stupendous. ֍ *Map E5*

8 Discovery Point

The full chill and hazards of Antarctic exploration grip you in this superb hi-tech exhibition. Focusing on the heroic and tragic expeditions of Shackleton and Scott, this display uses original film footage as well as stunning modern images and interactive computer screens. The highlight is a tour of the Dundee-built boat *RSS Discovery*, the one that

Perth

Home of Golf

The coastal links around St Andrews are recognized as the birthplace of golf – the earliest record of the game being played here dates to 1457. Golfing heritage continues in the city to this day, and St Andrew's Royal and Ancient Golf Club remains the ruling arbiter of the game.

Glamis Castle

carried Scott and his companions on their ill-fated expedition. (While in Dundee check out the Contemporary Arts Centre on Nethergate for great exhibitions and its fine bistro-café.) ◈ *Dundee • Map E5 • www.rrsdiscovery.com • Easter–31 Oct: 10am–5pm daily (from 11am Sun); 1 Nov–Easter: 10am–4pm daily (11am Sun) • Adm*

9 Glamis Castle
A royal residence since 1372, this is a magical castle *(see p46)*. A mass of towers and turrets, ancient treasures and a link with Shakespeare's *Macbeth* – could you ask for any more in a castle?

10 Pitlochry
Set on the edge of a loch, amid hills and woodland, this tartan-and-tweed town has a long history of serving visitors. Its proximity to Perthshire's beauty spots and sporting estates was the original draw, but now it boasts a theatre with a fine reputation, as well as a fish ladder, where salmon leap up a series of pools to reach their spawning grounds. Good shops and great scenery – a perfect introduction to the joys of Scotland. ◈ *Map E4/5 • www.pitlochry.org.uk • Theatre (May–Oct): (01796) 484626; • Fish Ladder (free) & Visitor Centre (adm) Apr–Oct: 10am–5:30pm daily*

An East Coast Drive

Morning

🕐 If your budget allows, book ahead for dinner at the **Peat Inn** (Cupar) or the **Old Course** (St Andrews) – see p89 for both.

Leave Edinburgh around 9am, cross the Forth Road Bridge (80p toll) and visit **Deep Sea World** at North Queensferry *(see p85)*. The fish will enthral you, so allow at least 90 minutes here.

Follow the coast road to Kirkcaldy, Glenrothes and **Falkland**. Here, have some refreshment in the deliciously organic **Greenhouse Restaurant** before visiting Falkland Palace. Remember to see the Royal Tennis Court before you leave – it's unique.

You may be hungry by now, but resist, as it's only a short drive via Glenrothes and the A915 to Upper Largo, where the famous **East Neuk** begins. Every village from here on is enchanting. Lunch in **Elie** at the **Ship Inn** *(see p89)*.

Afternoon

From here it's pointless trying to advise you further because – as you continue along the coast to St Andrews, passing through **Pittenweem**, **Anstruther** and **Crail** – you are bound to become distracted by this medley of coastal idylls and end up doing your very own thing regardless.

But don't forget your reservation if you've booked dinner, and leave all the delights of St Andrews for another day. All this in just 95 miles (150 km)!

Left **Blair Castle** Right **Forth Rail Bridge**

Best of the Rest

1 Blair Castle
A bright white castle, impressive in terms of size, location and contents (the Bonnie Prince left his gloves and pipe here, *see p47*).

2 Dunkeld
A village of great charm and character, with its restored historic street, the noble ruins of its 14th-century cathedral and gorgeous riverside walks. ⚅ *Map E5*

3 Arbroath Abbey
Impressive ruins, but most famous for the "Declaration of Arbroath", Scotland's eloquent charter for independence, a copy of which is on show. ⚅ *Map E6 • Apr–Sep: 9:30am–6:30pm daily; Oct–Mar: 9:30am–4:30pm Mon–Sat (closed Thu pm & Fri am), 2–4:30pm Sun • Adm*

4 Forth Bridges
Two outstanding examples of engineering, one a red giant of Victorian muscle, the other a modern suspended thread. Best seen lit up at night. ⚅ *Map F5*

5 Glen Isla
Very picturesque glen noted for its rare plants. At the end, a former drove road climbs to give wonderful views from Monega Hill and Glas Maol. ⚅ *Map E5*

6 Glen Clova
A knife-cut glen of wild scenery. Drive to the end for the best walks, or plan a long trek to Lochnagar and Loch Muick – tough hiking, but sensational. ⚅ *Map E5*

7 Scottish Fisheries Museum
It's hard to believe just how fascinating boats, nets and fish can be. First-class overview of the history of the fish supper. ⚅ *Anstruther • Map F5 • (01333) 310628 • www.scottish-fisheries-museum.org • Adm*

8 Verdant Works
Voted "European Industrial Museum of the Year", this is an invigorating presentation of the jute industry, the material upon which Dundee founded its urban economy. ⚅ *Dundee • Map E5 • (01382) 225282 • www.verdantworks.com • Adm*

9 Killiecrankie
The combined attractions of a famous battle site and an idyllic river gorge. Admire the famous Soldier's Leap, but don't try it! Queen Victoria loved this spot (and she was famously hard to please). ⚅ *Pitlochry • Map E4/5*

Killiecrankie

10 Montrose Basin Wildlife Centre
Internationally-important tidal basin and mecca for seafowl and waders. In autumn 35,000 pink-footed geese stop here to refuel during their southward migration. ⚅ *Map E6 • (01674) 676336 • www.swt.org.uk • Adm*

Price Categories

For a three-course meal for one with half a bottle of wine (or equivalent meal), taxes and extra charges.

£	under £15
££	£15–£25
£££	£25–£35
££££	£35–£50
£££££	over £50

Left **Peat Inn** Right **Andrew Fairlie**

🏆10 Places to Eat and Drink

1 Glen Clova Hotel
Situated at the end of a lovely glen is this hotel and restaurant. A simple all-day menu provides such staples as haddock, venison and home-made pies, while slightly more elaborate dishes are served for dinner. ⊗ *Glen Clova, Nr Kirriemuir • Map E5 • (01575) 550350 • ££*

2 Old Course Hotel
Imbued with golfing heritage yet retaining a refreshingly light air, this is dining at its finest. Virtuoso chef Mark Lindsey and a wine list of 200 bins. Smart dress and tie preferred. ⊗ *St Andrews • Map F5 • (01334) 474371 • £££££*

3 The Peat Inn
Exceptional food and range of wine at the fairest prices. This restaurant is an enduring favourite *(see p65).* ⊗ *Cupar • Map F5 • (01334) 840206 • £££*

4 Castleton House Hotel
Cosy country house with bright dining room and a prestigious menu. Everything from marbled terrine of woodpigeon to mushroom polenta cake with bok choi. ⊗ *Glamis • Map E5 • (01307) 840340 • £££*

5 The But 'n' Ben
Within the white walls of this old fisherman's cottage seafood is the speciality, naturally enough (especially Arbroath Smokies, *see p65).* Also good venison and local produce.

⊗ *Auchmithie, Nr Abroath • Map E6 • (01241) 877223 • ££*

6 63 Tay Street
This restaurant is the talk of the town. Award-winning young chef Jeremy Wares serves nouvelle cuisine in a clean, minimalist setting. It tastes and looks as if every ingredient has been hand-picked. ⊗ *63 Tay St, Perth • Map E5 • (01738) 441451 • £££*

7 Andrew Fairlie
French cuisine of the highest calibre served amid dreamy 1920s décor *(see p65).* ⊗ *Gleneagles Hotel • Map F4 • (01764) 694267 • £££££*

8 Moulin Hotel
A much-cherished old hotel which serves food but is most famous for its smoke-lined bar and its own brewery next door (Moulin Light and Ale of Atholl). ⊗ *11–13 Kirkmichael Rd, Moulin, nr Pitlochry • Map E5 • (01796) 472196 • £*

9 Ship Inn
Plain no-nonsense food served in a converted boathouse overlooking the harbour of this much-photographed village. Bar below, bistro above. ⊗ *Elie, nr Anstruther • Map F5 • (01333) 330246 • £*

10 The Cellar
A seafood heaven off a courtyard behind the Fisheries Museum *(see opposite).* One meat dish, plus some of the best fish in Scotland *(see p65).* ⊗ *Anstruther, Fife • Map F5 • (01333) 310378 • £££*

Note: *Unless otherwise stated, all restaurants accept credit cards and serve vegetarian meals*

Left **Botanical Gardens** Right **Pollok House**

Glasgow

EDINBURGH MAY BE THE PRETTY SISTER, *but Glasgow has the more dynamic character, as exemplified by the outgoing and friendly Glaswegians. From the highs and lows of its past, the city has endured to reinvent itself today as a centre of culture, cuisine, shopping and entertainment. Magnificent buildings are scattered right across the city, while the patronage of wealthy collectors has ensured the exceptional quality of Glasgow's museums and galleries.*

🔟 Sights

1. Kelvingrove Art Collection
2. Gallery of Modern Art
3. City Chambers
4. Glasgow Cathedral and Necropolis
5. People's Palace
6. Museum of Transport
7. Science Centre
8. Glasgow Botanical Gardens
9. House for an Art Lover
10. Burrell Collection and Pollok Park

City Chambers

St Mungo,
Glasgow's founder

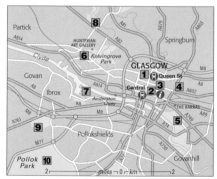

For up-to-the-minute information on Glasgow's attractions, check out **www.seeglasgow.com**

1 Kelvingrove Art Collection

The most visited collection in Scotland has paintings of inestimable value, including works by Botticelli, Giorgione *(The Adulteress brought before Christ)* and Rembrandt. Its outstanding representation of 17th-century Dutch and 19th-century French art is augmented by the home-grown talent of the Glasgow Boys and the Scottish Colourists. Note: the Kelvingrove Museum and Gallery will be closed for a major refit between 2003 and 2006; the best works from the collection will be on display at the McLellan Galleries. ◈ *McLellan Galleries, 270 Sauchiehall St • Map S2 • (0141) 565 4100 • 10am–5pm Mon–Thu & Sat; 11am–5pm Fri & Sun*

2 Gallery of Modern Art

Or, more correctly, a "Gallery of Astonishment". Some works are awesome and immediately grab your attention, others are deviously clever and quite a few are outrageously funny. A modern collection, then, that positively begs for mass appeal. Exhibits change frequently, but the ethos remains essentially the same.

Gallery of Modern Art

Let Patrick Hughes's *Shadow of War* trick your eyes, Eduard Bersudsky's *Titanic* intrigue your mind, and dare to stare down Peter Howson's fearsome mob, *Patriots*. Sebastião Salgado's excellent photographs are among the stand-out works on display. ◈ *Royal Exchange Sq • Map T3 • 10am–5pm daily (from 11am Fri & Sun) • Free*

3 City Chambers

"Palace" would be a more appropriate term, for this is the finest seat of any council in Britain, and Glasgow's most prestigious building. Modelled on Classical Italian architecture, the building was designed by William Young and completed in 1888. The exterior is dramatic enough, but the interior is an exercise in the excesses of lavish décor. Aberdeen granite, Carrara marble, mahogany, gold leaf, frescoes, mosaics, pillars and balustrades are combined to astonishing effect. The Banqueting Hall is surely modelled on a dandy's vision of heaven. ◈ *George Sq • Map U3 • (0141) 287 4018 • www.glasgow.gov.uk • By official tour only: 10:30am & 2:30pm Mon–Fri (phone to confirm)*

Kelvingrove Museum and Art Gallery by Kelvingrove Park

Though the art collection may have temporarily relocated, Kelvingrove Park is still an excellent place for a stroll, with great views

91

Glasgow Cathedral

4 Glasgow Cathedral and Necropolis

Immense and ancient, this cathedral was ranked by the Pope in 1451 as equal in merit to Rome as a place of pilgrimage. Founded around 1250 and completed a century later, it has been in continuous use since then and can boast original roof timbers. The choir screen is unique in Scotland, and the stained glass exceptional. On a hill to the cathedral's east looms the Necropolis, an extravagance of tombstones, crowned by a monument to John Knox *(see p11).* ❧ *Cathedral Square • Map V2 • (0141) 552 6891 • Apr–Sep: 9:30am–6pm Mon–Sat, 1–5pm Sun; Oct–Mar: closes 4pm daily*

5 People's Palace

Typically Glaswegian, this is a museum of ordinary life. Nothing fancy or outstandingly old, but a fascinating insight into how the average family lived, worked and played in the not-so-distant past. The Winter Gardens are connected to the museum and make a tranquil spot to rearrange your thoughts. ❧ *Glasgow Green • Map V1 • (0141) 554 0223 • www.seeglasgow.com • 10am–5pm daily (from 11am Fri & Sun)*

6 Museum of Transport

Bicycles, cars, lorries, buses, trains, fire engines … hundreds and hundreds of everything on wheels in acres of gleaming metalwork. You can walk through or climb into the larger vehicles, or sit in an original Glasgow tram. Upstairs are 250 model ships illustrating the story of Clyde shipbuilding. Watch out for the penny on the cobbles of the re-created 1938 shopping street – but don't try to pick it up, or you could be there all day. ❧ *1 Bunhouse Road • Map U1 • (0141) 287 2720 • www.seeglasgow.com • 10am–5pm daily (from 11am Fri & Sun)*

7 Science Centre

Myriad puzzles, experiments and demonstrations to entertain and inform. There's also an IMAX screen and a revolving tower – a sensational place *(see pp18–19).*

8 Botanical Gardens

Positively bulging with greenery and colour, these gardens are a favourite with locals and visitors alike. The highlights

Science Centre

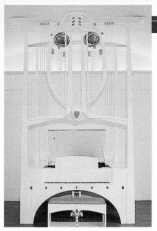

Mackintosh piano, House for an Art Lover

are the glasshouses – the main structure named Kibble Palace – famous for their orchids and tropicana *(see p51)*.

9 House for an Art Lover

In 1901 Glasgow's tour-de-force architect, Charles Rennie Mackintosh, and his decorative artist wife, Margaret Macdonald, entered a magazine competition to design a "House for an Art Lover". It was to be "… a grand house, thoroughly modern, fresh and innovative…" Their exquisite vision remained just a design until 1989 when, authentic to the smallest detail, the building and its contents were created.

Ⓢ *Bellahouston Park, Dumbreck Rd • Map U2 • (0141) 353 4770 • www.house foranartlover.co.uk • 1 Apr–30 Sep: 10am–4pm Sun–Thu, 10am–3pm Sat • Adm*

10 Burrell Collection and Pollok Park

One of the world's great private collections, this is a dazzling and eclectic array of art and artifacts. The presentation is superb in a purpose-designed building surrounded by a wooded parkland. If you see nothing else in Glasgow, this is the one to go for *(see pp16–17)*.

A Full Day in Glasgow

Morning

🕐 Leave at 9:30am and buy a First Day Ticket for Tourists (£4 unlimited travel on First buses from 9:30am to midnight). Purchase the ticket as you board a No. 45 bus to the **Burrell Collection**. Allow two hours to take in the scope of this amazing museum, and make sure you see the Old Masters paintings.

Return to the city centre and take a 66 or 41 (every 10 mins) to the **Botanical Gardens**. (If you do this tour on Fri or Sun, reverse the order and visit the Botanics first as the Burrell won't be open until 11am)

📍 Lunch at the gardens, either with a picnic in the grounds or at one of the many cafés along the **Byres Road**, opposite the Botanics entrance.

Afternoon

Take one of the many buses heading back into the centre of Glasgow, and get off at **Sauchiehall Street**. Walk and shop your way along, taking a right at Buchanan Street. Call in for coffee at the **Princes Square** shopping centre *(see p94)*, a great place to watch people. Continue on to the **Gallery of Modern Art** *(see p91)* – this gallery has plenty of light-hearted works and gives, rather than takes, energy.

Finally, stroll through George Square and admire the **City Chambers** before dining at one of the many restaurants in the Merchant City neighbourhood, such as **Babbity Bowster**, **Café Gondolfi** or **City Merchant** *(see p95)*.

Left **Emblem at St Mungo Museum** Centre **Tenement House** Right **Glasgow School of Art**

🔟 Best of the Rest

1 St Mungo Museum of Religious Art

Excellent overview of the world's religions through their art. Best of all is Salvador Dali's *Crucifixion*, a unique perspective. 🔊 *2 Castle St • Map V2 • (0141) 553 2557*

2 Waverley Excursions

Experience the past on the world's last sea-going paddle steamer. An inspiring way to travel. 🔊 *Anderston Quay • Map V1 • (0845) 130 4647 • www.waverleyexcursions.co.uk*

3 Hunterian Art Gallery

Another great gallery, best known for its Rembrandts, its virtual monopoly on the 19th-century genius of Whistler and the Mackintosh House. 🔊 *82 Hillhead St, nr Kelvingrove Pk • Map V1 • (0141) 330 5431 • www.hunterian.gla.ac.uk • Free*

4 Tenement House

Tenements were standard Glasgow flats and Agnes Toward lived an ordinary life in this one for over 50 years. Nothing has been changed. 🔊 *145 Buccleuch St • Map S1 • (0141) 333 0183 • Adm*

5 M & D's Scotland's Theme Park

A massive adventure park with all the jaw-clenching thrills of the fairground. Rides to suit all ages and nerves *(see p60)*.

6 Princes Square

Luxurious shopping centre in a renovated square of 1841 – the genteel atmosphere is heightened by the occasional appearance of a piano player. 🔊 *48 Buchanan St • Map T3*

7 Sharmanka Kinetic Gallery

Eduard Bersudsky makes performing contraptions from junk, and this is his extraordinary theatre. 🔊 *2nd floor, 14 King St • Map U3*

8 Glasgow School of Art

Still a working college, this is Charles Rennie Mackintosh's most famous building. 🔊 *167 Renfrew St • Map S2 • (0141) 353 4526 • Visits by official tour only*

9 Citizens Theatre

An internationally famous venue for performances of classics. Two modern studios complement the old Victorian auditorium. 🔊 *119 Gorbals St • Map V1 • (0141) 429 0022 • www.citz.co.uk*

10 The Barras

A market full of silver-tongued vendors and piles of bargains, not all of them entirely legal. Riotously alive and fascinating, but hold on tight to your wallet. 🔊 *54 Calton Entry • Map V1 • Sat & Sun*

M & D's Scotland's Theme Park

Price Categories

For a three-course meal for one with half a bottle of wine (or equivalent meal), taxes and extra charges.

£	under £15
££	£15–£25
£££	£25–£35
££££	£35–£50
£££££	over £50

Left **Rogano** Right **City Merchant**

Places to Eat and Drink

1 Amaryllis
Glasgow's best, in terms of food and rarefied atmosphere. Since 2001, the menu has felt the guiding hand of Britain's top chef, Gordon Ramsay. For this level of cooking, Amaryllis is very good value. 🔊 1 Devonshire Gdns, off Great Western Rd • (0141) 337 3434 • £££££

2 Ubiquitous Chip
On a cobbled road in the West End stands this home to 30 years of culinary excellence. Always a champion of Scottish produce, this is Glasgow at its most endearing. 🔊 12 Ashton La, off Byres Rd, Hillhead • Map U1 • (0141) 334 5007 • ££££

3 Stravaigin
Where the nation's fish, beef, lamb and game are mixed with the world's sauces, herbs and spices. Eclectic mix of flavours, but Stravaigin's judicious touch wins the day. 🔊 28–30 Gibson St, Hillhead • Map U/V1 • (0141) 334 2665 • £££

4 Firebird
Popular hangout for drinks and great pizzas – simple and consistently good. 🔊 1321 Argyle St, nr Museum of Transport • Map U1 • (0141) 334 0594 • ££

5 Fratelli Sarti
Very Italian. Lively, crowded and displaying a genuine love of food in a living, breathing, everyday sense. Restaurant on Bath St, with a café and deli round the corner. 🔊 121 Bath St/133 Wellington St • Map T2 • (0141) 204 0440 • ££

6 St Jude's
Elegant retreat for Glasgow's modish people. Loungy in the bar, while the restaurant gains plaudits by the score for its invention and exemplary quality (Pacific rim and European flavours). 🔊 190 Bath St • Map S2 • (0141) 352 8800 • ££££

7 Rogano
A wonderful place to imbibe, in equal measure, splendid cocktails and the Art Deco surrounds. Expensive in the main restaurant but fresh seafood a bargain in the brasserie. 🔊 11 Exchange Pl, off Exchange Sq • Map T3 • (0141) 248 4055 • £££–££££

8 City Merchant
Looking like it's been around for aeons (though only in fact since the late 1980s), City Merchant is a Gallic-Scottish delight. Alongside some meaty mains, fish is the star. 🔊 197 Candleriggs • Map U3 • (0141) 553 1577 • £££

9 Café Gondolfi
Café in the broadest sense: breakfast, coffee, afternoon tea and all main meals and snacks in between. A seasonal evening menu scampers the larders of Europe. 🔊 64 Albion St • Map U3 • (0141) 552 6813 • ££

10 Babbity Bowster
Stout white building with a welcoming Scottish interior that evokes a distant rural life. Great pub and restaurant with rooms (see also p146). 🔊 16 Blackfriars La • Map U3 • (0141) 552 5055 • ££

Note: Unless otherwise stated, all restaurants accept credit cards and serve vegetarian meals

Left **Wallace Monument** Centre **Loch Lomond** Right **Arduaine Gardens**

North and West of Glasgow

THIS BUCOLIC REGION BECAME THE FOCUS of Scotland's first tourist industry in early Victorian times, and, with Loch Lomond and the Trossachs National Park at its splendid centre, that allure remains as strong today. In the west are the rocky peaks of the Isle of Arran and a seaboard of fjord-like lochs, where a mild climate supports some splendid gardens. In the east stands Stirling – a key town in the country's warring past – its mighty clifftop castle overlooking lush farmland. Here, William Wallace and Robert the Bruce fought for independence, a battle eventually won within sight of the castle on the field of Bannockburn.

Sights

1 Bannockburn Centre
2 Wallace Monument
3 Stirling Castle
4 Blair Drummond Safari Park
5 Loch Lomond and the Trossachs National Park
6 Inveraray Castle
7 Arduaine Gardens
8 Crarae Gardens
9 Rothesay Castle, Bute
10 Brodick Castle, Arran

Statue of Robert the Bruce at Stirling Castle

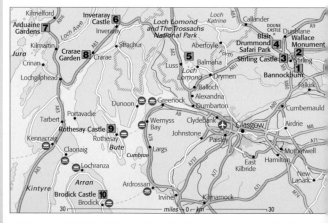

1 Bannockburn Heritage Centre

The site of the decisive battle in 1314 (see p32) is marked by a visitor centre and an arresting equestrian statue of Robert the Bruce. At the centre, kids can try on helmets and chainmail, and enter Bruce's cave to meet the fabled spider who inspired him to renew his fight. ◈ Map F4 • Site open all year • Heritage Centre: 10:30am–4pm daily (10am–6pm in summer) • Adm

Stirling Castle Grand Battery

2 Wallace Monument

Erected in 1869, this 75-m (250-ft) tower commemorates William Wallace and his valiant fight for Scotland's independence. The climb to the top takes in Wallace's two-handed broadsword, but most electrifying of all is the "talking head", which presents Wallace's defence before his brutal execution in 1305. Splendid 360-degree views from the top. ◈ Map F4 • 10am–4pm (until 5pm in summer) daily • Adm

3 Stirling Castle

A commanding rock-top castle, concealing architecture of an exceptional quality, most notably the restored Great Hall and the Royal Palace (see also p46). ◈ Map F4 • (01786) 450000 • Apr–Sep: 9:30am–6pm daily; Oct–Mar: 9:30am–5pm daily • Adm

4 Blair Drummond Safari Park

As if elephants, rhinos, zebras, giraffes, lions, meerkats and ring-tailed lemurs weren't enough, you can also see your first lechwe (unless, of course, you're already au fait with these African antelopes). Beyond the animal life, this is also a terrific play centre, with a giant Astraglide, a Flying Fox and pedalos for getting to Chimpanzee Island. ◈ Map F4 • (01786) 841456 • www.safari-park.co.uk • Mar–Sep: 10am–5.30pm daily • Adm

5 Loch Lomond and the Trossachs National Park

The broad, friendly mountains and poetic scenery of Scotland's first national park are ideal for the casual walker and watersport lover. Luss is the prettiest village. It hosts a popular Highland Games (see pp58–9) in June and has a welcoming tea shop or two. Cruises run from here, and from Balloch, Tarbet and Balmaha. ◈ Loch Lomond Shores Visitor Centre • Map F4 • (01389) 721500 • www.lochlomondshores.com

Trossachs National Park

For a fabulous place to stay by the shores of Loch Lomond see Cameron House (p147)

The Wonderful World of Crarae Gardens

Lady Grace Campbell laid out the gardens in the 1920s, making exciting use of plant specimens that her nephew Reginald Farrer brought back from his travels to Tibet and the Himalayas. On the higher ground is the forest-garden, a feature found nowhere else in Britain, where over 100 tree species grow under forest conditions on their own plots. Crarae is of international importance and a member of "Glorious Gardens of Argyll and Bute" (www.gardens-of-argyll.co.uk).

Arduaine Gardens

6 Inveraray Castle

Despite the ravages of fire, clan Campbell's family seat is a splendid pseudo-Gothic palace with pointed towers marking its corners. It was built for the Duke of Argyll in 1745. The lavish interiors were designed by Robert Mylne and contain Regency furniture and priceless works of art. The Armoury was stocked to fight the Jacobites and is an awesome display of weaponry. If you have time (it's about a 90-minute round trip) walk to the hilltop folly in the grounds.

◈ Map F3 • (01499) 302203 • www. inveraray-castle.com • Jul & Aug: 10am–5:45pm Mon–Sat (Sun 1–5:45pm); Mar–Jun & Oct: closed Fri • Adm

7 Arduaine Gardens

A dazzling assembly of rhododendrons, azaleas, magnolias and hosts of exotics from the Pacific Islands to the Himalayas. Arduaine is beautifully situated on a promontory between sea lochs, and glories in the warm winds from the Gulf Stream (see p51).

8 Crarae Gardens

You don't have to be a rhododendron specialist to be bowled over by this beautifully manicured orchestration of colour. An outstanding and rare collection, which is at its best in spring (see p51).

9 Rothesay Castle, Bute

By virtue of its age, design and deep-water moat (one of only two remaining in Scotland), this is a remarkable medieval castle. Built around 1098 in the days of Norse occupation, it was restyled in the 13th century and

Inveraray Castle

fitted with high curtain walls and drum towers. Its circular court-yard is a curious feature and unique in Scotland. Bute itself is a mere 35-minute crossing from Wemyss Bay – north of Largs on the A78 – to Rothesay Bay; an even shorter crossing is from Colintraive to Rhubodach, on the north coast of the island.
⊗ Map F3 • (01700) 502691 • Apr–Sep: 9:30am–6:30pm daily; Oct–Mar: 9:30am–4:30pm Mon–Thu & Sat (closed Thu pm), 2–4:30pm Fri & Sun • Adm

10 Brodick Castle, Arran
Originally a Viking keep before the Dukes of Hamilton claimed it, this 13th-century fortified tower was extended by Oliver Cromwell and then trans-formed into a stately home in Victorian times. The last Hamilton moved out only in 1957. A solid red sandstone building with fanciful trimmings, it contains a noted collection of silver, por-celain and paintings. The gardens are beautifully maintained (try to catch the rhododendrons in spring bloom), as are the woodland trails. The main ferry to Arran (just under an hour) is from Ardrossan, on the mainland coast, just north of Irvine. ⊗ Map G3 • (01770) 302202 • Castle open 25 Mar–27 Oct: 10am–5pm daily; Park open all year: 9:30am–sunset daily • Adm

Brodick Castle

A Day in the Trossachs

Morning

🕐 Reserve your morning cruise on the **SS Sir Walter Scott** (Tel (01877) 376316) in advance, and note that it does not run on Wednesdays.

Leave Glasgow by 8:45am, driving north on the A81 to Strathblane and Aberfoyle. You are now in the scenic and famous **Trossachs**. Park at the Trossachs Pier for your 11am cruise on **Loch Katrine**, a gorgeous secluded loch.

You arrive back at 12:45pm and a short drive takes you to Kilmahog (great name, but the Woollen Mill is pretty touristy), so pass it by unless you're overly curious about knitwear. Head on to **Callander** for lunch, where there's plenty of choice, or buy delicious pies at the Scotch Oven, a superb baker, and picnic by the river.

Afternoon

Carry on to Doune, Dun-blane and Bridge of Allan. There are many tempta-tions en route – castle (see p100), safari park, motor museum – and you may fall by the way.

If not, however, aim to be at the **Wallace Monument** before 4pm. The slice of history here is extremely palatable, accompanied by panoramic views of the area, including the craggy heights of **Stirling Castle**.

Finally, wend your way up into moorland for dinner at **Bouzy Rouge** (see p101). Either head back to Glas-gow or go further east to stay at Edinburgh or St Andrews (about an hour's journey to each by car).

Around Scotland – North and West of Glasgow

Left **Kilchurn Castle** Centre **Bonawe** Right **Oban**

TOP 10 Best of the Rest

1 Kilchurn Castle

Hauntingly atmospheric ruins of a Campbell castle, built in 1440 on an island in Loch Awe. Visible from many vantage points, or you can go there by boat. ✆ *Map E3*
• *Boat trips (01866) 833333* • *Open access*

2 Oban

Busy harbour town best viewed from McCaig's Folly. Many local attractions and ferries to Mull, Coll, Colonsay, Tiree and the Western Isles. ✆ *Map E3*
• *Tourist Info (08707) 200630*

3 Doune Castle

Often used in film sets, this 14th-century castle has a magical air. Most enchanting is the Lord's Hall, with its musicians' gallery, double fireplace and oak screen.
✆ *Map F4* • *(01786) 841742*

4 Hollow Mountain Power Station

Tunnels and huge underground caverns house this massive hydro-electric plant. Like a science-fiction set, it is fascinating and rather weird. ✆ *Nr Lochawe* • *Map E3*
• *(01866) 822618* • *Easter to mid-Nov: 9:30am–5pm daily (to 6pm in Aug)* • *Adm*

5 Bonawe Historic Iron Furnace

The best-preserved charcoal-fuelled ironworks in Britain. Learn how iron was made here in 1753 in this lovely setting by Loch Etive.
✆ *Taynuilt* • *Map E3* • *(01866) 822432*
• *www.historic-scotland.net* • *Apr–Sep: 9:30am–6:30pm daily* • *Adm*

6 Crinan Canal

Take a stroll along this scenic 9-mile (16-km) canal, completed in 1801 and now used by yachts and fishing boats. The best places to see them are at Ardrishaig, Cairnbaan or Crinan. ✆ *Map F3*

7 Auchindrain Township

A novel outdoor museum of restored thatched cottages and outbuildings, showing the past styles of West Highland life. ✆ *Nr Inveraray* • *Map F3* • *(01499) 500235*

8 Scottish Crannog Centre

The little-known and ancient art of building *crannogs* (defensive homesteads built on stilts in lochs) has been rediscovered here at Loch Tay. Beware – underwater archaeologists at work. ✆ *Kenmore*
• *Map E4* • *(01887) 830583*

9 Kintyre

Paul McCartney sang about this glorious peninsula which has miles of beaches, a top golf course (Machrihanish) and the ethereal cave crucifixion painting on Davaar Island. ✆ *Map G3* • *Tourist Info (08707) 200609*

10 Kilmartin Glen

Inhabited for 5,000 years, this glen has a phenomenal concentration of archaeological remains: standing stones, temples and burial cairns. Pause at Kilmartin Church to see the best collection of early Christian crosses. ✆ *Map F3*

Price Categories

For a three-course meal for one with half a bottle of wine (or equivalent meal), taxes and extra charges.

£	under £15
££	£15–£25
£££	£25–£35
££££	£35–£50
£££££	over £50

Left **Creagan House** Right **Loch Fyne Oyster Bar**

Top 10 Places to Eat and Drink

1 The Roman Camp

Voluptuous curtains, deep sofas and blazing fires make this country hotel a delight, and the restaurant excels. Their guinea fowl breast with truffle noodles is a winner. *Callander • Map F4 (01877) 330003 • ££££*

2 Chatters

Unnoteworthy in appearance or location, but excellent food. Bar menu and à la carte in a cottage atmosphere. Eat outside in summer. *58 John St, Dunoon • Map F3 • (01369) 706402 • Wed–Sat only, lunch and dinner • £–£££*

3 Loch Fyne Oyster Bar

Long-established in this converted stone cattle byre, the oyster bar offers two vegetarian dishes daily and an ocean of the freshest seafood. Bring a hearty appetite and have a go at the lobster platter. *Cairndow, nr Inveraray • Map F3 • (01499) 600236 • £££*

4 The Drover's Inn

A flagstone floor, cobwebbed walls and a menagerie of stuffed animals to fight your way past – it's quite an experience. Pub grub and beer flow all day. *Inverarnan, on Loch Lomond • Map F4 • (01301) 704234 • £*

5 Cromlix House

Distinguished restaurant showcasing the best of Scottish produce. Small choice, but cooked to perfection. *Kinbuck, By Dunblane • Map F4 • (01786) 822125 • ££££*

6 Bouzy Rouge at the Sheriffmuir Inn

This middle-of-nowhere former coaching inn is now a trendy restaurant well worth crossing the moor to find. Nothing exotic, but good food at good prices. *Nr Bridge of Allan & Dunblane • Map F4 • (01786) 823285 • £££*

7 Airds Hotel

The Michelin star first stopped overhead in 1990, and this country hotel restaurant hasn't looked back since *(see p65)*. *Port Appin, Appin • Map E3 • (01631) 730236 • ££££*

8 Creagan House

Winning awards left, right and centre, this converted 17th-century farmhouse is a secret about to break. From quail to local lamb, this is good food at a surprisingly low price. *Strathyre • Map F4 • (01877) 384638 • ££*

9 Tigh-an-Truish

Old-world inn by the famous "Bridge over the Atlantic". Historic and wonderful, you still expect pirates to breeze in. Real ale and delicious pub grub. *Clachan, Isle of Seil • Map F3 • (01852) 300242 • ££*

10 Kilmartin House Café

An adjunct of the Kilmartin Museum, this light-lunch café is mainly vegetarian but does excellent venison burgers. Home baking and great coffee. *Kilmartin • Map F3 • (01546) 510278 • £*

Note: *Unless otherwise stated, all restaurants accept credit cards and serve vegetarian meals*

Left **Cawdor Castle's drawbridge** Right **Fort George**

Grampian and Moray

THE NORTHEASTERN CORNER OF SCOTLAND – *a veritable medley of landscapes* – is home to equally diverse industries, from the traditions of farming, fishing and distilling to the the more recent business of North Sea oil extraction. The high granite massif of the Cairngorms is Scotland's prime centre for mountain sports. Then comes the forested splendour of Royal Deeside – Queen Victoria's beloved retreat – and the quilted fields of Buchan's rich farmland. Along the river Spey is the heartland of whisky production, while on the coast are beaches, cliffs and enchanting fishing villages.

Sights

1. Aberdeen
2. Dunottar Castle
3. Pitmedden Garden
4. Fyvie Castle
5. The Whisky Trail
6. Balmoral Castle and Royal Deeside
7. Cairngorms
8. Cawdor Castle
9. Fort George
10. Moray Coast Villages

Carrbridge, near the Cairngorms

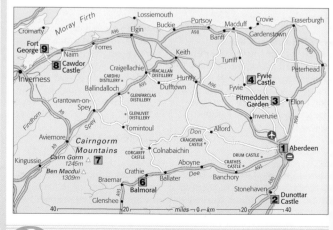

Aberdeen
1 The "Granite City" has beautiful buildings, year-round floral displays and a long beach fringed with entertainments, including the Beach Leisure Centre *(see p61)* and the Stratosphere, a science discovery complex. Provost Skene's House (once home of a 17th-century provost, or mayor, of Aberdeen) is the oldest building, dating from 1545, while Marischal College is one of the world's largest granite edifices. The Maritime Museum (charting the nautical world from ship-building to ship wrecks) is outstanding, as is the Art Gallery, which mixes temporary contemporary shows with a collection spanning the 18th–20th centuries. ◈ *Map D6 • Stratosphere, 179 Constitution St (01224) 640340 • Maritime Museum, Shiprow (01224) 337700 • Art Gallery, Schoolhill (01224) 523700 • Provost Skene's Ho, Guestrow (01224) 641086*

King's College, Aberdeen

Dunottar Castle
2 Few castles can match Dunottar's magnificent setting – it stands heroically isolated on a stupendous rock – and few castles have endured such intense bombardments. In 1651, while harbouring the Scottish regalia (which were secretly smuggled out by a brave woman), it withstood an eight-month siege by the English. It's dungeons, too, have witnessed exceptional sufferings and deaths. 800 years of attack have taken their toll, but Dunottar remains an almost mythical sight, especially at sunrise. ◈ *Nr Stonehaven • Map E6 • (01569) 762173 • Easter–Oct: 9am–6pm Mon–Sat, 2–5pm Sun; Nov–Easter: 9:30am–sunset Fri–Mon (closed mid-week) • Adm*

Pitmedden Garden
3 The striking patterns and symmetry of the formal Great Garden is like no other. Originally laid out in 1675, the elaborate floral designs were meticulously recreated. The effect is stunning. Also here are idyllic pond and wildlife gardens, and a Museum of Farming Life *(see p51)*. ◈ *Map D6*

Pitmedden Garden

For more information on Aberdeen, check out the city's website: www.aberdeencity.gov.uk

Balmoral

4 Fyvie Castle

Dating from 1390, this formidable building is one of the finest examples of Scottish Baronial architecture. Its life through the ages is testified by the mix of contemporary panelling, 17th-century plasterwork and a treasure trove of collectable paintings. Be sure to visit the restored 18th-century walled garden, which specializes in Scottish fruit and vegetables. ◈ Nr Turriff • Map D6 • Late Mar–end Jun & Sep–Oct: noon–5pm Sat–Wed; Jul & Aug: 10am–5pm daily • Adm

5 The Whisky Trail

Seven of Scotland's finest malt whisky distilleries invite you inside. Apart from the magic of

Speyside cooperage sign

the shining copper stills, the once-secretive process of whisky-making is revealed, enthusiasm infused and *uisge beatha* ("water of life") consumed (see p31).

6 Balmoral and Royal Deeside

Bordering the salmon pools of the River Dee, Queen Victoria bought this castle – her "dear paradise" – in 1852. Balmoral remains the holiday home of the monarch to this day and, consequently, the rolling countryside around the banks of the river has taken on the royal moniker. Cast an eye round the castle's sumptuous ballroom, then make the most of the enchanting forest walks. ◈ Map D5 • (01339) 742334 • www.balmoralcastle.com • Apr–31 Jul: 10am–5pm daily • Adm

Victoria and Albert's Balmoral

It was the riverside setting that Victoria fell in for in 1848 when she first visited Balmoral. And it was her husband Albert who worked with the Aberdeen-born architect William Smith to create the white granite palace that replaced the old castle and stands here still, a medley of fantastical turrets typical of the Baronial style.

7 Cairngorms

A superb range of mountain peaks surrounded by pine forests and lochs. Ideal for testing walks, lively watersports and inspiring scenery (see pp30–31).

8 Cawdor Castle

A private home, handed down through the generations since the time when Macbeth lived here ... or so legend has it.

Full of history and delight, creepy relics, magnificent trees and a garden maze *(see also p47)*.
Ⓧ *Nr Nairn • Map D4 • (01667) 404615 • May–Oct: 10am–5pm daily • Adm*

9 Fort George
On a peninsula jutting into the Moray Firth is this vast fort complex, built at enormous expense 250 years ago and still used as an army barracks today. Immensely impressive defences now guard a vintage armoury. Check out the special summer events *(see p25)*.

10 Moray Coast Villages
These charming communities thrived in the herring boom of the 19th century, but today only Lossiemouth, Buckie (with its excellent Drifter Museum), Macduff and Fraserburgh continue as fishing ports. Crovie (pronounced "crivie") is the pick of the bunch. Access is by foot only, its picturesque street strung out below cliffs – a fabulous walk. The walk to Gardensown is an adventure for the sure-footed *(see pp62–3)*. Findhorn – famous for its spiritual community – is beautifully located on a sandy lagoon. A tour of the coastal road (highly recommended) will reveal a dozen other villages, each with its own unique character to divine. Ⓧ *Map C5–6*

The Moray Coast

A Day's Driving Tour

Morning

🕘 Leave **Aberdeen** around 9am and drive on the A93 through Deeside's splendid scenery to Crathie, where you'll find **Balmoral Castle** opening its gates. If, however, you're outside Balmoral's short opening season *(see p104)*, then visit **Crathes** or **Drum Castle** instead – less famous, but equally impressive *(see p106)*.

Return to **Ballater**, which you passed through on the way, but take the B976 on the south of the river. The **Station Restaurant** does all-day meals, anything from a bacon sandwich or pain au chocolat to a three-course meal.

Afternoon

While browsing the shops in Ballater, Look out for royal insignias: they indicate the Queen's favourite establishments.

From Ballater find the A939 and drive north on a twisting road. The terrain is wild, heathery moorland and mountainous. The road takes you past quaint and lonely **Corgarff Castle**, and on to **Tomintoul**, one of the highest villages in Scotland. From here, take the B9008 to the distillery of **Glenlivet** for a tour of their whisky-making vats, stills and barrels, and a tasting. Tours last about 40 minutes; the tastings, unfortunately, much less.

Spend the night around **Dufftown** or **Keith** with a view to driving to Portsoy and taking the coast road either east or west the next day. About 90 miles (150 km) in total.

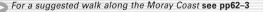

For a suggested walk along the Moray Coast **see pp62–3**

Left **Brodie Castle** Centre **Elgin Cathedral** Right **Dallas Dhu Distillery**

TOP10 Best of the Rest

1 Moray Firth Dolphins
This is the only known resident population (they number around 130) of bottlenose dolphins in the North Sea. 🕸 *Map D4 • Info Centre: North Kessock (01349) 868542 • Boat trips: (01463) 717900; (01381) 600323; (01381) 620958.*

2 Craigievar Castle
A delicate tower house with the grace and detail of porcelain. Scottish Baronial style at its best, and with some lovely monkey-puzzle trees in the grounds *(see p47).*

3 Drum Castle
One of the three oldest surviving tower houses in Scotland, its High Hall unchanged since medieval times. In fact, it has been owned by just one family for 653 years! 🕸 *Nr Banchory • Map D6 • (01330) 811204 • www.drumcastle.org.uk*

4 Crathes Castle
Another exemplary tower house of the 16th century, with original features in the Great Hall. Wonderful topiary in the ancient yew hedge. 🕸 *Banchory • Map D6 • (01330) 844525*

5 Brodie Castle
Majestic Z-Plan tower house, which has survived many attacks and contains a treasury of furniture and paintings. Catch it in spring when 400 species of daffodils are in glorious bloom. 🕸 *Forres, nr Nairn • Map D4 • (01309) 641371*

6 Duff House Gallery
This astonishingly secret offshoot of the National Galleries of Scotland is housed in an exquisite Georgian mansion. The collection includes works by Scottish greats Ramsay and Raeburn, as well as El Greco. 🕸 *Banff • Map C6 • (01261) 818181 • www.duffhouse.com*

7 Elgin Cathedral
Once known as "the Lantern of the North", this cathedral was burned out of spite by the Wolf of Badenoch in 1390, but its ruins still draw a crowd. 🕸 *Map C5 • (01343) 547171*

8 Dallas Dhu Distillery
When this working distillery closed it was preserved as a time capsule of whisky-making between 1898 and 1980. Beautifully done, and with a traditional free dram! 🕸 *Forres, nr Nairn • Map C5 • (01309) 676548*

9 Stonehaven
Quaint seaside resort with a harbour, an open-air Olympic-size swimming pool and a giant, playable draughts (checkers) board. Birds wheel and soar around the cliffs and Dunottar Castle *(p103)* is a short drive away. 🕸 *Map E6*

10 Kildrummy Castle
The once "noblest of northern castles" is now a grandiose ruin. Brilliant in terms of design and construction, it retains many unique 13th-century features. 🕸 *Nr Alford • Map D5 • (01975) 571331*

Information on many of Scotland's castles, churches and houses can be found at www.nts.org.uk and www.historic-scotland.com

Price Categories

For a three course meal for one with half a bottle of wine (or equivalent meal), taxes and extra charges.	£ under £15
	££ £15–£25
	£££ £25–£35
	££££ £35–£50
	£££££ over £50

Left **Ardoe House** Right **Crynoch Restaurant**

Places to Eat and Drink

1 Ardoe House
Granite mansion with an up-market restaurant. A la carte or table d'hote menus prepared by a much-lauded chef. ❧ *South Deeside Rd, Blairs, Aberdeen • Map D6 • (01224) 860600 • £££*

2 Tullich Lodge
Family-run village pub, full of character and homeliness – and terrific food. People travel far to eat here; top marks for value. ❧ *Main St, Newburgh, north of Aberdeen • Map D6 • (01358) 789444 • ££*

3 Milo's
With a menu that reflects the crossover of a French-trained local chef, Milo's reputation is set to rocket. From high teas to the finest à la carte dinner, the fantastic meals are served in a tiny restaurant overlooking the harbour. ❧ *2 Crook 'O'Ness St, Macduff • Map C6 • (01261) 831222 • £££*

4 Crynoch Restaurant
Rustic décor and a Bavarian chef delivering modern cuisine with flair. Specialities such as venison with fresh local chanterelles or grilled wood pigeon salad grace the menu. ❧ *Lairhillock Inn, Netherley, By Stonehaven • Map E6 • (01569) 730001 • www.lairhillock.co.uk • £££*

5 Fagins
Seafood is the speciality in this charming harbour village eatery. Great Sunday lunches and special deals (Wed & Thu). ❧ *Whitehills (nr Banff) • Map C6 • (01261) 861321 • ££*

6 The Lemon Tree
Funky arts centre with bistro-bar. The best music venue in the northeast region. Live bands play at weekends. ❧ *5 West North St, Aberdeen • Map D6 • (01224) 642230 • Closed Mon • £*

7 Silver Darling
One of the best restaurants in the country, this is a seafood emporium with Aberdeen harbour spread out before you *(see p64)*. ❧ *Pocra Quay, Aberdeen Harbour • Map D6 • (01224) 576229 • ££££*

8 The Shore Inn
An ale house with atmosphere, right by the harbour. Bar food served all day in summer and at weekends in winter. The place where the locals eat and drink. ❧ *48 Church St, Portsoy • Map C5 • (01261) 842831 • £*

9 The Old Monastery
Superb little hilltop restaurant with short opening hours, so phone in advance. French-style food with panache. ❧ *Nr Buckie • Map C5 • (01542) 832660 • Wed–Sat: lunch & dinner; First Sun of each month: lunch only • £££*

10 Archiestown Hotel
A Speyside hotel that's popular with fishermen. Its bistro has earned a good reputation, and wild salmon is a regular speciality. Vegetarians should give advance notice. ❧ *Main St, Archiestown, nr Craigellachie • Map D5 • (01340) 810218 • Feb–Sep only • £££*

> **Note:** Unless otherwise stated, all restaurants accept credit cards and serve vegetarian meals

Left **Loch Ness and Urquhart Castle** Centre **Culloden Battlefield** Right **Inverewe Gardens**

The Highlands

THE NAME ALONE EVOKES THOUGHTS *of mountains, heather, bagpipes, castles, clans, romance and tragedy. And, indeed, the Highlands has it all. It is the combination of peerless scenery, enduring traditions and a sense of nostalgia (albeit for a rather idealized past) that gives the Highlands their irresistible allure. True, the weather is not always great, but rain brings out the best in waterfalls and adds artistic touches of mist! It's a sparsely inhabited region, where you may still find single-track roads and more sheep than people. Life takes on a slower pace, and often hotels and restaurants work shorter hours, but the great compensation is peace. Little wonder that so many aspects of the Highlands have been adopted as symbols of the nation as a whole.*

 Sights

1. Inverness
2. Culloden Battlefield
3. Loch Ness
4. Ben Nevis and Fort William
5. Glencoe
6. Glenfinnan Monument and Jacobite Steam Train
7. Ardnamurchan
8. Eilean Donan Castle
9. Torridon
10. Inverewe Gardens

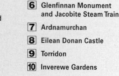

Glenfinnan Monument

Previous pages **Eilean Donan Castle**

1 Inverness

A city in name but a bustling town by nature, Inverness is redeemed from the blight of its shamefully dull modern architecture by the majestic red sandstone castle (now the court house), fine old houses and the beauty of the River Ness. Inverness Museum and Art Gallery invites "hands on the Highland Heritage" (but you have to leave the artifacts behind), and the Aquadome is a fun-packed swimming centre. The Islands Walk is sublimely peaceful. ◈ Map D4
• Tourist Info: Castle Wynd (01463) 234353 • Museum & Gallery: Castle Wynd; Open Mon–Sat; Adm • Aquadome: Bught Park (01463) 667501; Open daily; Adm

2 Culloden Battlefield

16 April, 1746 – the last battle to take place on British soil and defeat for Bonnie Prince Charlie and the Jacobites (see pp32–3). The slaughter by the "Bloody Butcher's" (the Duke of Cumberland's) Hannoverian army was quick and brutal. The battlefield is gradually being restored to its appearance at the time of the bloodshed. To walk here among the graves of the clans is still a peculiarly emotional experience. The story is well told and illustrated in the visitor centre.
◈ Map D4 • Visitor Centre: (01463) 790607; www.nts.org.uk • 25 Mar–27 Oct: 9am–6pm daily; 28 Oct–24 Mar: 10am–4pm daily • Adm

Culloden Battlefield

3 Loch Ness

Ice Age glaciers gouged out a deep trench along a split in the land mass of Scotland, and the resulting valley is known today as the Great Glen. Loch Ness is its cause célèbre, with arresting views, the mystery of its reclusive monster and the evocative ruins of Urquhart Castle. Do not eschew a visit to the great loch! (See pp24–5.) ◈ Map D4

4 Ben Nevis and Fort William

Britain's highest mountain is 1,343m (4,406 ft) high and makes a great walk under good conditions (see p40). But the peak is frequently shrouded in mist, and the drive up Glen Nevis offers a more reliable reward, taking you to a lovely waterfall. Fort William lies below the mountain and is a major shopping town with plenty of attractions (see p24). Its West Highland Museum has many Jacobite relics, and Treasures of the Earth exhibits glittering heaps of gems. ◈ Map E3
• Tourist Info: Cameron Sq, Fort William (01397) 703781 • West Highland Museum: Open year-round • Treasures of the Earth: Closed throughout Jan

Ben Nevis and Fort William

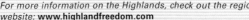

Glencoe

5 Glencoe

A rugged mountain range gathered into gorgeous scenery through which the twisting main road seems to creep submissively. A favourite skiing, mountaineering and walking area, and infamous for the terrible 1692 massacre of clan MacDonald *(see pp26–7)*.

6 Glenfinnan Monument and Jacobite Steam Train

Another memorial to the Jacobite uprising led by Bonnie Prince Charlie *(pp32–3)*, this time on the site where his campaign began. Here, a visitor centre explains the history. The monument is impressive, but the chief attraction is

Eilean Donan Castle

Return of the Bonnie Prince

Set on reclaiming the British Crown for the Stuart line, Bonnie Prince Charlie landed on the west coast of Scotland in 1745 with but a handful of men. His temerity, as well as widespread support for the Jacobite cause, won over many Scots, and when he came to raise his standard at Glenfinnan, numbers swelled as clans such as the Camerons rallied to his side.

getting here – the scenery en route is stunning. Take time to marvel at the nearby viaduct (featured in the *Harry Potter* film) and wait for a passing steam train – even better, be in a passing steam train. ◉ *Map E3 • Visitor Centre: (01397) 722250; Late Mar–Oct: 10am–5pm daily; Adm • Jacobite Steam Train (01463) 239026; mid-Jun to early Oct*

7 Ardnamurchan

This peninsula – with its rugged backbone of mountains, pretty villages and what is one of the most delightful roads in the country, ending in a parade of white sand – is as lyrical in nature as it is in name. Acharacle is a famed den of musicians (try the hall or Glenuig Inn), while Glenmore is home to a highly innovative Natural History Centre with a "living building". Wild deer sometimes graze on its roof. From Kilchoan you can catch a ferry to Tobermory on Mull. ◉ *Map E2 • Tourist Info: (01397) 703781; www.ardnamurchan.com • Natural History Centre: (01972) 500209; Apr–Oct*

8 Eilean Donan Castle

No one manages to drive past this castle without leaping for their camera. Small, beautiful and magical, the restored 13th-century fortress of clan Macrae stands on an island in magnificent scenery on the road to Skye *(see also p47)*. ◎ *Map D3 • mid-Mar–Oct: 10am–5pm daily; Nov: 11am–4pm daily • Adm*

9 Torridon

Just when you think mountains can't get any better, you come to Torridon! Flanked by a long sea loch, the red sand-stone buttresses of Beinn Alligin, Ben Dearg, Liathach (the highest, *see p41*) and Beinn Eighe rise up into arresting outlines. From Little Diabaig you can walk a delightful coastal path to Alligin Shuas, or to Craig *(see p62)*. The National Trust runs

Torridon

an informative Countryside Centre with nearby herds of red deer and Highland cattle. ◎ *Map D3 • Countryside Centre • (01445) 791221 • www.nts.org.uk • 1 May–29 Sep: 10am–6pm daily • Adm*

10 Inverewe Gardens

A west coast phenomenon, these much-vaunted gardens are worth travelling a long way to see. The sheer richness and variety of plant life growing in what many consider to be a cold wilderness is a tribute to a plant enthusiast's vision, hard work, nature's bountifulness and warm Atlantic winds *(see p51)*.

A Highland Day Trip

Morning

Pack a picnic in **Inverness**. There are lots of marvellous picnicking possibilities on this route, so it would be a shame not to take one.

Leave Inverness by 10am to make the best of the day, taking the B852 to Dores and drive along the south side of **Loch Ness** – a beautiful and much quieter road than that on the northern shore. Try to stop off at the **Foyers Falls** *(see pp62–3)*.

Enjoy the hill-country drive to **Fort Augustus**, and pop in for a coffee at the bustling **Lock Inn**, right beside the canal. Walk along the canal to view Loch Ness from the shore behind the old abbey.

Drive along the A82 on the north side of Loch Ness, (stop at Invermoriston to view the river pools and old bridge) and visit **Urquhart Castle**. Have your picnic lunch here.

Afternoon

Your picnic will, hopefully, have recharged your batteries sufficiently for a visit to one of the **Loch Ness Monster visitor centres** in Drumnadrochit – fascinating, and rather persuasive.

Refill your thermos in Drum-nadrochit, then take the A831 to Cannich, and the minor road to **Glen Affric**.

Enjoy an hour's walk in this renowned beauty spot, before returning to the bustle of Inverness via Kilmorack and the south shore of the **Beauly Firth**. A round trip of 115 miles (185 km).

For suggested walks in the Highlands see pp42–3

113

Left **Dunrobin Castle** Centre **Plockton** Right **Coast at Lairg**

🔟 Best of the Rest

1 Dunrobin Castle
A home befitting its wealthy landowners, the dukes of Sutherland. Towers, turrets and a palatial interior upon which no expense has been spared. Garden falconry displays too. ◈ Golspie • Map C4 • (01408) 633177 • Adm

2 Glen Affric
Glen of outstanding beauty, most easily accessed from the east at Cannich. But at the western end, near Morvich, there's a walk to the breathtaking Falls of Glomach (see p25). ◈ Map D3

3 Ullapool
Delightful grid-plan village with Gaelic street names, boat trips, ferries to the Western Isles, a museum and the dream-world Assynt Mountains. Visit Corrieshalloch Gorge en route. ◈ Map C3

4 Plockton
Prime candidate for Scotland's prettiest west-coast village, Plockton has sea, palm trees, a Rare Breeds Farm and occasional folk music sessions at the harbourside inn. ◈ Map D3

5 Hydroponicum, Achiltibuie
A Garden of Eden without the dirt. You'll be amazed at what's grown in this glasshouse using a soil-free irrigation system to keep the plants fed (see p51).

6 Gairloch Heritage Museum
A leader of its kind, this local exhibition excels with a programme of old-industry demonstrations, such as weaving, dyeing and butter-churning. By so doing, the museum brings history back into the life of the present. Terrific fun! ◈ Achtercairn • Map C3 • (01445) 712287 • www.gairlochheritagemuseum.org.uk • Adm

7 The Road to Applecross
To get to this small coastal village, you'll drive on pure adrenalin – the road climbs 750 m (2,000 ft) in steep zig-zags to the Pass of the Sheep. Even they have to hold on tight. The scenery – with views across to Skye – is magnificent, and from here the more gradual descent into Applecross begins. ◈ Map D2

8 Timespan
Well worth a visit to understand the effect of the 19th-century Clearances, which even today is visible throughout the north. ◈ Helmsdale • Map C5 • (01431) 821327 • www.timespan.org.uk • Adm

9 Dornoch Cathedral
Madonna chose it for her wedding and 16 earls of Sutherland requested it for their burials. An impressive 13th-century cathedral (now the parish church). ◈ Map C4

10 Lairg
The annual event here is the one-day sheep sale – the biggest in the country with up to 40,000 sheep. ◈ Map C4 • Mid-Aug • Tourist Info (summer only): (01549) 402160

Price Categories

For a three-course	£ under £15
meal for one with half	££ £15–£25
a bottle of wine (or	£££ £25–£35
equivalent meal), taxes	££££ £35–£50
and extra charges.	£££££ over £50

Off the Rails, Plockton

Places to Eat and Drink

1 Inverlochy Castle
Many culinary awards have been bestowed upon the restaurant of this prestigious hotel. Three dining rooms, a lavish set menu (Modern British cuisine) and a lengthy wine list. ✆ *Torlundy, Fort William • Map E3 • (01397) 702177 • £££££*

2 Old Pines
Conscientiously organic, devoted to sourcing local ingredients, a member of the "Slow Food" movement and with its own smokehouse, this little restaurant has earned a big name. Set no-choice menu, everything beautifully cooked and presented. ✆ *Spean Bridge • Map E3 • (01397) 712324 • ££££*

3 Culloden House
Another luxurious hotel dedicated to the highest refinements of eating and drinking. Cream of watercress and apple soup sets the impeccable standard. ✆ *Inverness • Map D4 • (01463) 790461 • ££££*

4 Eden Court
A simple dining area offering light meals at Inverness's vibrant theatre. Bright and breezy for lunch or pre-theatre meals. ✆ *Bishop's Rd, Inverness • Map D4 • (01463) 225585 • ££*

5 Seagreen
A much-loved restaurant focused on local, organic, wholefood and seafood – but also a bookshop and complementary therapy centre. Sustenance for mind, body and soul. ✆ *Kyle of Lochalsh • Map D3 • (01599) 534388 • ££*

6 Summer Isles Hotel
A no-choice set menu "strives for perfection" and frequently succeeds. Advance bookings only, and vegetarian dishes by arrangement. Gourmet dining in a spectacular setting. ✆ *Achiltibuie, Ross-shire • Map C3 • (01854) 622282 • ££££*

7 The Ceilidh Place
Hotel-restaurant-bar and vibrant entertainments venue. Everything from a snack to a feast, plus live music and dance aplenty. ✆ *14 West Argyle Street, Ullapool • Map C3 • (01854) 612103 • £££*

8 Clachaig Inn
A legendary haunt of walkers, this hotel offers a wide range of food but is best known for its bar – as essential to Highland trekkers as a first munro. ✆ *Glencoe • Map E3 • (01855) 811252 • ££*

9 Off the Rails
The atmosphere in this old railway station is delightful, and the food exquisite. Plenty of choice, and adequate wine – supreme value. ✆ *Plockton • Map D3 • (01599) 544423 • ££*

10 Café na Lusan
Vegetarian and vegan-friendly, this café serves delicious, wholesome organic food, as well as a mix of wines and beers – internet access too. ✆ *Craigard Rd, Oban • Map E3 • (01631) 567268 • No credit cards • £*

Note: *Unless otherwise stated, all restaurants accept credit cards and serve vegetarian meals*

Jura

West Coast Islands

MORE THAN 600 ISLANDS LIE SCATTERED *along Scotland's Atlantic coast-line, from seabird clustered eyots to the land masses of Skye, Mull, Lewis and Harris. The West Coast Islands represent escapism at its best and amply repay the effort of reaching them with the distinctive lifestyles and hospitality of island folk. Regular ferries run all year, and special "island-hopping" fares are available.*

Left **Callanish Stone Circle, Isle of Lewis** Right **St Martin's Cross, Iona**

🔟 Sights

1. Jura
2. Islay
3. Colonsay and Oronsay
4. Mull
5. Iona and Staffa
6. Coll
7. Small Isles
8. Skye
9. Barra
10. Isle of Lewis

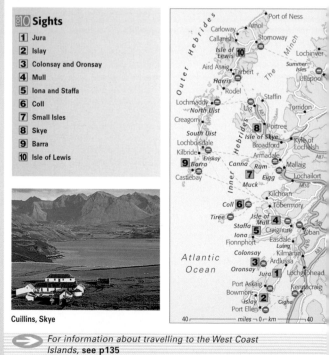

Cuillins, Skye

For information about travelling to the West Coast Islands, see p135

Harbour, Colonsay

1 Jura

The wildest and least visited of the Hebridean islands. Overrun by red deer and dominated by its central hills, the Paps, Jura has been little affected by modernity: a single road links the ferry port and the main settlement, Craighouse. If you revel in solitude, the walks are tremendous. ⊗ *Map F2 • Tourist Info: (08707) 200617*

2 Islay

A thriving island with eight distilleries producing peaty malts. Bowmore, the island's capital, has an unusual circular church, designed to deprive the devil of corners to hide in! And Britain's most impressive 8th-century Celtic cross can be found at Kildalton. More than 250 species of birds have been recorded on Islay's varied landscapes. ⊗ *Map F2–G2 • Tourist Info: (08707) 200617 • www.isle-of-islay.com*

3 Colonsay and Oronsay

Colonsay has provided farmland and shelter to people since at least the Bronze Age, and many of their tombs and standing stones remain. Old traditions persist here, and Colonsay is still a strong crofting *(see p119)* and fishing community. Wild flowers and birds thrive on this terrain, but it is the coastline, with its mix of sprawling and secretive beaches, that lures most visitors. Check the tides and walk out to the adjacent little island of Oronsay, with its ruined priory; its Christian roots go back as far as Iona's. ⊗ *Map F2 • Tourist Info: (08707) 200630 • www.colonsay.org.uk*

4 Mull

Matching Skye for beauty if not for size, Mull is the second largest of the Inner Hebrides. Don't miss the prize gardens at Torosay Castle (which can be reached by miniature railway from Craignure), while the imperious Duart Castle is a more austere proposition. A tour of the island must include side trips to Iona and Staffa, and Calgary Beach will stop you in your tracks. Tobermory is the place to unwind – its colourful seafront is a classic postcard scene. The Misnish Bar there often has live music. ⊗ *Map E2–F2 • Tourist info: (08707) 200610*

Duart Castle, Mull

> *George Orwell stayed at a remote cottage on Jura in 1946 to work on his final novel,* Nineteen Eighty-Four; *for more, see pp44–5*

Fingal's Cave

industrialist; you can visit his incredible fantasy home, Kinloch Castle, as well as wander the island's towering mountains. Eigg was a landmark community buyout, and the islander-owners now run a crafts shop and tours. Their ceilidhs *(see p59)* are legendary! The Sgurr of Eigg, a sugar-loaf spur, yields fabulous views.
✎ *Map D–E2 • Tourist Info: (01687) 462170*

5 Iona and Staffa

Iona is a sparkling island of white sand beaches with an active crofting community. Visitors come in their hundreds daily in summer to visit the famous restored abbey (avoid 10am–4pm for a chance of peace). It was here that Columba came in 563 to establish a missionary centre *(see p32)*. Staffa contains Scotland's greatest natural wonder: Fingal's Cave, formed by thousands of basalt "organ pipes", which inspired Mendelssohn to compose his famous *Hebrides Overture*. ✎ *Map F2 & E2*
• Boats for Staffa leave from Fionnphort
• Tourist Info: (08707) 200630.

6 Coll

Wild flowers, migrant birds, otters, standing stones, active crofts, a castle and a surfeit of beaches contribute to making this a particularly varied and delightful island.
✎ *Map E2 • Tourist Info: (08707) 200630.*

7 Small Isles

While Canna and Muck are home to traditional farming communities, Rum was once the private playground of a rich

8 Skye

Mountainous, misty and magical, Skye is an island of dramatic scenery, with an ancient castle, an idolized distillery and plenty more attractions *(see pp20–21)*.

9 Barra

This small isle encapsulates all the charm of the Hebrides: scintillating beaches, the culture of the Gaels, tranquillity and road-priority to sheep. No matter how you arrive, it will make a deep impression: planes land on the sands of Cockle Beach, while ferries sail into a delightful bay where the 11th-century Kisimul Castle poses on an island of its own. A soothing place to unwind.
✎ *Map D1 • Tourist Info: (01851) 703088*

Rum

→ For a perfect retreat from (the comforts of) modern life, found on the island of Coll, **see p44**

Barra

10 Isle of Lewis

Although geographically one island, the northern half is called Lewis and the southern half, Harris. Together, they are world-famous for producing tweed. One thing you absolutely must see in Lewis is the spectacular 4,500-year-old stone circle of Calanish, which resonates with a deep sense of spirituality. Arnol has an engaging traditional "black-house" (blackened by smoke) and Carloway a fine stone fort. Harris is more mountainous. Drive the "Golden Road" for the best scenery, and stop at Luskentyre beach, where you could imagine you were in Australia. ✆ *Map C2 • Tourist Info: (01851) 703088*

Crofting

Crofts are unique to the High-lands and Islands. They are small parcels of agricultural land, worked in addition to other sources of income. There are around 17,000 today, and grants now ensure their continuation. But in the mid-19th century, crofters were denied basic rights and suffered great abuse and hardship at the hands of unscrupulous landlords.

A Day Around Mull

Morning

🕐 Book both your Staffa boat trip (Tel 0800 783 8470) and your car reservation for the Caledonian Mac-Brayne ferry (Tel (01631) 566688) in advance.

Depart Oban on the 7:45 am Calmac ferry to **Craignure** on Mull (45-minute crossing).

Drive to Fionnphort to catch the 9:45 trip to **Staffa** (10:45 on Sat). This takes 40 minutes each way and you have one hour on Staffa to walk among puffins and visit the awesome **Fingal's Cave**, the basalt rock formation that so inspired Mendelssohn.

On your return to Fionnphort, leave your car and take the quick ferry crossing to **Iona**. Have lunch in the **Argyll Hotel** (a particularly good vegetarian selection).

Afternoon

Climb the hill above the abbey. The longer you leave your visit to the **abbey** the less crowded it will be. Iona is too beautiful and serene to rush, and you may want to spend the rest of the day wandering its shores and rugged terrain, contem-plating this small island's historical significance.

If not, return to Craignure in time to visit **Torosay Castle** and its fine gardens. Try to get there before 4pm to make the visit worthwhile.

Note: If you don't have a car, you can do most of this tour, in summer, by boat from Oban – call the 0800 number above.

Left **Sunset, Inner Hebrides** Right **Luing**

⏱0 Best of the Rest

1 Arran
Long a favourite of Glaswegians, Arran is often described as "Scotland in miniature". Goat Fell is its craggy core, while the surrounds of Brodick Castle offer more urbane, forest-path walks. ◈ Map G3 • Tourist Info: (01770) 302401

2 Tiree
Well-established on the surfers' circuit, this flat island not only boasts some of the finest Atlantic rollers on its beaches but it also claims the highest number of sunshine hours in Britain. ◈ Map E1 • Tourist Info: (08707) 200630

3 The Uists and Benbecula
A string of islands connected by causeways, with huge expanses of beaches on the west and rocky mountains on the east. Aside from the scenery, this is also a wonderful trout fishing area. ◈ Map C1–D1 • Tourist Info: (01851) 703088

4 Gigha
Exceptionally fertile island ("Isle of God"), which produces gourmet cheeses and a remarkable abundance of tender plants and flowers, especially in the much-acclaimed Achamore Garden. ◈ Map G2 • Tourist Info: (08707) 200609

5 Eriskay
Real-life scene of the *Whisky Galore* wreck in 1941, this is the dream island of the Hebrides. Beaches, crofts, hills – everything is how the romantic would have it. ◈ Map D1 • Tourist Info: (01851) 703088

6 Easdale
This former slate quarry has been transformed into a picturesque village. Surrounded by holes and fragmented rocks, it is bizarre and fascinating – a living museum. ◈ Nr Oban • Map E3 • Tourist Info: (08707) 200630

7 Summer Isles
As inviting as their name sounds, this small cluster of islands in Loch Broom offers solitude before the magnificent arena of the Coigach mountains. ◈ Map C3 • Tourist Info: (01854) 612135

8 Kerrera
A popular place for yachts to berth, this green, hilly island is ideal for walking, with clear views to Mull and the finest outlook on Oban. ◈ Map E3 • Tourist Info: (08707) 200630

9 Lismore
Situated in splendid scenery, this once important church island is now a quiet holiday retreat. Very green and fertile, it's name is said to mean "great garden". ◈ Map E3 • Tourist Info: (08707) 200630

10 Luing
As it is not famous for anything except its defunct slate quarry, you should have this isle to yourself. Pretty, and easy to tour by bicycle. ◈ Nr Isle of Seil • Map F3 • Bicycle hire: (01852) 314256

Previous pages **The Isle of Skye**

Price Categories

For a three course meal for one with half a bottle of wine (or equivalent meal), taxes and extra charges.

£	under £15
££	£15–£25
£££	£25–£35
££££	£35–£50
£££££	over £50

Three Chimneys

🔟 Places to Eat and Drink

1 Three Chimneys
Shirley and Bill Speirs have been enhancing their international reputation for 20 years in this sublime cottage restaurant *(see also p64)*. ◈ *1 Colbost, Glendale, Skye • Map D2 • (01470) 511258 • www.threechimneys.co.uk • ££££*

2 Bonaventure
Chef Richard Leparoux has chosen the remotest corner to set up his restaurant. Well worth the trek to find dazzling French-Scottish dishes in an old RAF base with picturesque surrounds. ◈ *Aird, Uig, Isle of Lewis • Map C2 • (01851) 672474 • £££*

3 Port Mor House
Dinner is included with bed and breakfast here, simply because there's nowhere else to go. Thankfully the restaurant excels itself *(see also p45)*. ◈ *Port Mor, Isle of Muck • Map E2 • (01687) 462365 • ££*

4 Kilmichael Country House
Considering the hotel's five-star rating, its restaurant is a bargain. Set four-course menus and a connoisseur's wine list. Booking essential. ◈ *Glencloy, Brodick, Isle of Arran • Map G3 • (01770) 302219 • www.kilmichael.com • £££*

5 Eilean Iarmain Hotel
Charming and cosily set in a huddle of historic buildings by the sea (with its own oyster beds). Highest quality set four-course menu (three choices for each course) and elite wine list. ◈ *Isle Ornsay, Sleat, Skye • Map D2 • (01471) 833332 • www.eileaniarmain.co.uk • £££*

6 The Mishnish
Celebrated pub on Tobermory's colourful seafront. Always bustling (and often packed) with locals and visitors. Regular live music. ◈ *Main St, Tobermory, Mull • Map E2 • (01688) 302009 • £*

7 An Tuireann
Swish, modern arts exhibition centre. Part of the draw is the delicious vegetarian meals and snacks served in the café. ◈ *Struan Rd, Portree, Skye • Map D2 • (01478) 613306 • 10:30am–4:30pm Mon–Sat • £*

8 Jura Hotel
Quaint old coastal hotel. In any one evening you are likely to meet most of Jura's inhabitants. Simple food in the scenery of the gods. ◈ *Craighouse, Jura • Map F2 • (01496) 820243 • £*

9 Castlebay Bar
A rollicking bar with cheap meals … or silver service and all the trimmings in its restaurant overlooking the village bay. ◈ *Castlebay, Barra • Map D1 • (01871) 810223 • £ (bar) • £££ (restaurant)*

10 Druimard Country House Hotel
Dining room in a meticulously restored Victorian house situated just opposite Mull Theatre and overlooking the glen. ◈ *Dervaig, Mull • Map E2 • (01688) 400345*

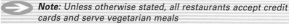

Left **Mousa Broch, Shetland** Centre **Skara Brae, Orkney** Right **Scapa Flow Visitor Centre**

The Far North

DON'T LET THE REMOTENESS DETER YOU, *for it is the very emptiness itself that commends upon the visitor senses of wonder and privilege in the Far North. The dazzling beaches along the northern coastline are a surprise to many, while further north still are the former Viking strongholds of Orkney and Shetland. Orkney is green and fertile, and contains one of the greatest concentrations of prehistoric remains in Europe. Shetland is wilder, with millions of seabirds and islanders who celebrate their Viking roots with a blazing fire festival.*

Ring of Brodgar, Orkney

🔟 Sights

1. Handa Island
2. Cape Wrath
3. Caithness Glass, Wick
4. Old Man of Hoy, Orkney
5. Maes Howe, Orkney
6. Kirkwall, Orkney
7. Skara Brae, Orkney
8. Jarlshof, Shetland
9. Mousa Broch, Shetland
10. Hermaness National Nature Reserve, Shetland

Earl's Palace, Kirkwall

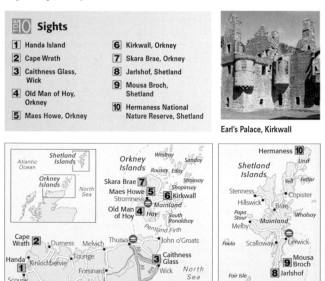

Handa Island

1 Handa Island

Once populated by hardy people who elected a queen and ran their own parliament, Handa was evacuated when the potato crop failed in 1847. Now it is only seabirds that live here – and what a fantastic colony! Of particular note are the belligerent arctic and great skuas, kittiwakes, razorbills and the largest assembly of guillemots (66,000) in Britain. A ferry from Tarbet will take you to this dramatic island. ◈ Map B3
• Ferry: (01463) 714746; mid Apr–mid Sep

2 Cape Wrath

This is the most north-westerly point on the British mainland. Perched high on a clifftop stands a Stevenson lighthouse (1827); below, the ocean pounds the rocks in a mesmerizing display of the Atlantic's strength. Five miles (8 km) eastwards at Clo Mor are the highest cliffs on mainland Britain (281 m / 900 ft). The cape is reached by ferry from the Cape Wrath Hotel, and a minibus runs to the lighthouse in summer. ◈ Map B3 • Ferry: (01971) 511376

3 Caithness Glass, Wick

Watch orange globules of molten glass grow at the hands of skilful blowers. With the highest quality of glass, crystal engraving and craftmanship, the products of Caithness Glass are celebrated around the world. To view production, go during the working week. ◈ Map B5 • (01955) 602286 • www.caithnessglass.co.uk • Easter–Dec: Glass-blowing, 9am–4:30pm Mon–Fri; Visitor Centre, 9am–5pm Mon–Sat & 11am–5pm Sun

4 Old Man of Hoy, Orkney

This sandstone pinnacle rising 150 m (500 ft) from the sea is the most famous stack in Britain. It seems constantly to change colour as the light varies, and never fails to mesmerize. Impressively, climbers have scaled its precipitous face. The Scrabster–Stromness ferry deviates to give passengers a view, but its best angle is from land. Hire bikes at Moaness and cycle to Rackwick Bay (on the way visit the Dwarfie Stane, a hollow rock), then it's a 2-hour round-trip on foot. ◈ Map A5 • Bike hire at Moaness: (01856) 791225

Old Man of Hoy

For places to stay on Orkney and Shetland see p150

century and still going strong. Nearby are the ruins of the bishop's and earl's palaces. The town museum is excellent, and many shops sell an extensive range of Orcadian jewellery. ⊗ Map A5 • Tourist Info: (01856) 872856 • Palaces: (01856) 871918; summer only; adm • Museum: (01856) 873191; free

St Magnus's Cathedral, Kirkwall

5 Maes Howe, Orkney

This magnificent burial chamber, built c.2700 BC, is a World Heritage Site. Stoop low and walk through the entrance tunnel, carefully aligned with the solstice sun, and enter the greatest concentration of Viking graffiti ever discovered. Norsemen plundered the treasure but left the walls with a wealth of runes describing the kind of boasts and grumbles that men still make today. The torchlit tour is absolutely spellbinding! ⊗ Map A5 • (01856) 761606 • Apr–Sep: 9:30am–6:30pm daily; Oct–Mar, 9:30am–4:30pm Mon-Sat, 2–4:30pm Sun • Adm

6 Kirkwall, Orkney

The capital of Orkney is an endearing town of twisted streets, ancient buildings and the constant comings and goings of ferries. Most striking of all is the enormous red and yellow St Magnus's Cathedral, built in the 12th

Skara Brae

7 Skara Brae, Orkney

Another World Heritage Site, and one that predates the Egyptian pyramids. In 1850, a storm revealed some ruins in the sands. Archaeologists excavated and were astonished to find a 5,000-year-old Stone Age village, which had been abandoned so suddenly that most of the rooms and furnishings were left intact. Today, you can see the stone beds and sideboards of these Neolithic people, and discover how and what they cooked. A visitor centre explains all. ⊗ Map A5 • (01856) 841815 • Late Mar–end Sep: 9:30am–6:30pm daily; Oct–Mar: 9:30am–4:30pm • Adm

8 Jarlshof, Shetland

This outstanding warren of underground (but roofless) chambers represents not one period of settlement but at least five. The oval-shaped houses are Bronze Age; the Iron Age added the broch (see Mousa Broch) and wheelhouses; the Picts established their own dwellings; the Vikings erected long houses, and a farm was created in medieval times. You can't beat a good building site and this one, close to the soaring bird-cliffs of Sumburgh head, is exceptional. ⊗ Map B1 • (01950) 460112 • Apr–Sep: 9:30am–6:30pm daily • Adm

Jarlshof

9 Mousa Broch, Shetland

Around 500 BC the Iron Age people began building defensive forts called brochs. Masterfully designed, these double-skinned walls of dry stones were raised into circular towers, with an elegant taper at their waists. Remains of brochs are scattered across northern Scotland but Mousa is the best preserved. You can only reach it by boat, and then must climb 13 m (43 ft) to the open parapet. ✎ *Map B2*
• *Tourist Info: (01595) 693434 • Boat trips (01950) 431367; Apr–Sep daily*

10 Hermaness National Nature Reserve, Shetland

When you look from here to Muckle Flugga lighthouse, you're gazing at the northernmost tip of Britain. Aside from the view, the cliff-edged reserve is a favourite breeding ground for bonxies (great skuas). Alongside these pirates (they steal food from other gulls), there are gannets, razorbills, red-throated divers and Shetland's largest gathering of tammy nories (puffins). ✎ *Unst • Map A2*
• *(01595) 693345 • Best times to visit are mid-May–late Jul & mid-Sep–early Oct*

A Day on Orkney

Morning

🕐 Start the morning from the flagstoned village of **Stromness** and head out on the road to **Skara Brae**. The roads turn and undulate on rolling pasture and are really a network of lanes, but the way is well signposted – a pity in some respects, as Orkney is a delightful place to get lost in.

You'll need two hours to do the Neolithic remains justice, as well as fitting in a visit to **Skaill House** and sampling cakes dripping with icing in the café.

Drive on to the great stone circle known as the **Ring of Brodgar**, and also visit the roadside standing stones of **Stenness**.

🍴 So far you've only covered 12 miles (20 km)! Time for lunch over at the **Maes Howe Visitor Centre**.

Afternoon

After lunch, explore **Maes Howe**. It's dark inside, and a guide lights up the runes with a torch. Drive on to **Kirkwall**. Visit the cathedral (it has a great little café) and the museum – neither of which are arduous or lengthy – and walk the town's charming streets.

🍴 In the evening, dine at the **Creel Inn & Restaurant** *(see p129)* in St Margaret's Hope and feel like a satiated Viking.

Note, Orkney is a delightful place to cycle and it's easy to hire bicycles. The car route described above makes a lovely day's cycle ride if you return to Stromness after Maes Howe.

Left **Smoo Cave** Right **Stromness**

Best of the Rest

1 Eas A'Chual Aluinn Fall, nr Kylesku
Britain's highest waterfall drops 200 m (650 ft) at the end of Loch Glencoul. ◉ *Map B3 • Take a boat from Kylesku, Mar–Oct: (01971) 502345*

2 RSPB Forsinard Reserve
The great peatland here, known as the Flow Country, offers walks among rare plants, insects and birds. ◉ *Map B4 • (01641) 571225 • www.rspb.org.uk*

3 Smoo Cave, Durness
Remarkable natural cavern beside the sea. You can walk in a little way, but it's best to take a floodlit boat tour. Easily Scotland's best underground sight. ◉ *Map B4 • (01971) 511259.*

4 Swanson Art Gallery, Thurso
Hosting touring exhibitions of surprising quality, the Swanson has a widely varying programme. ◉ *Map B5 • (01847) 896357*

5 Scapa Flow Visitor Centre, Hoy, Orkney
An exploration of the bay of Scapa Flow, where, in 1917, the

Italian Chapel, Orkney

captive German Navy scuttled 74 ships. ◉ *Map A5 • (01856) 791300*

6 Churchill Barriers and Italian Chapel, Orkney
Impressive causeways built in World War II by Italian prisoners of war, who were also responsible for the exquisite chapel. ◉ *Lamb Holm, nr Kirkwall • Map A5 • Chapel open daily, dawn to dusk*

7 Stromness, Orkney
A town of flagstoned streets and a museum that draws on the Orcadian connection with the Hudson Bay Shipping Company. ◉ *Map A5 • Tourist Info: (01856) 850716*

8 Balfour Castle, Orkney
Stay here if you can, but if not at least visit. Guided tours of this delightfully idiosyncratic home are possible during the summer. Not daily, so phone ahead *(see p45)*. ◉ *Shapinsay • Map A5*

9 Ring of Brodgar, Orkney
A marvellously atmospheric prehistoric site of 36 slabs raised to form a circle. There are taller (but fewer) standing stones nearby at Stenness. ◉ *Nr Stromness • Map A5 • Tourist Info: (01856) 850716*

10 Fair Isle, Shetland
Famous for knitted patterns and as a haven of traditional crafts, this remote island has awesome cliff scenery and birdlife. The ferry is weather-dependent, so be prepared for a wait. ◉ *Map B1 • www.fairisle.org.uk*

Price Categories

For a three-course	£ under £15
meal for one with half	££ £15–£25
a bottle of wine (or	£££ £25–£35
equivalent meal), taxes	££££ £35–£50
and extra charges.	£££££ over £50

Busta House

🔟 Places to Eat and Drink

1 Tongue Hotel
A characterful old hotel, the low prices of which belie the quality of exotic Highland fare served. Treat yourself to corn-fed chicken stuffed with garlic, or Caithness venison sausages. ✪ *Tongue • Map B4 • (01847) 611206 • ££*

2 Port-na-Con, nr Durness
Lochside restaurant which offers international cuisine. Incredible variety and value, and adequate wine list *(see also p149).* ✪ *Loch Eriboll, nr Durness • Map B4 • (01971) 511367 • ££*

3 Eddrachilles Hotel, Scourie
Among trees on a ragged coastline, this fine old hotel has a stone-walled dining room where local smokehouse food is served. A long conservatory too for catching the sun. ✪ *Badcall Bay, Scourie • Map B3 • (01971) 502080 • ££*

4 Kinlochbervie Hotel
Somewhat stark, but it more than makes up for it through good views and simple value-for-money food. Hill lamb, venison, salmon and local seafood are favourites. Surprisingly good wines. ✪ *Kinlochbervie • Map B3 • (01971) 521275 • ££*

5 Dunnet Head Tea Rooms
The UK's most northerly mainland tearoom with a cornucopia of home baking. ✪ *Dunnet Head; from Thurso take the coast road east • Map B5 • Easter–Sep: noon–3pm & 6–9pm (closed Wed) • No credit cards • £*

6 Cape Wrath Hotel
Family-run landmark on this stunning stretch of coast. Hugely popular with fishermen, maybe because the restaurant serves mainly game. No culinary fanfares, just honest food in a friendly atmosphere. ✪ *Nr Durness • Map B3 • (01971) 511212 • ££*

7 Pierowall Hotel, Orkney
Come here for the best fish and chips in the isles – probably in Scotland. Nothing fancy but simple home-cooking and plenty of choice. ✪ *Pierowall, Westray • Map A5 • (01857) 677472 • ££*

8 Creel Inn, Orkney
Multi-award-winning seafront restaurant in a timeless stone village. Imaginative cooking with Orcadian produce – try the wolf-fish broth. ✪ *St Margaret's Hope • Map A5 • (01856) 831311 • £££*

9 Weisdale Mill, Shetland
In this renovated old mill, combine the visual delights of the Bonhoga Gallery with delectable snacks: marinated herring, smoked salmon, organic quiches – it's all praiseworthy. ✪ *Weisdale • Map B1 • 11am–4pm; closed Mon • No credit cards • £*

10 Busta House, Shetland
Historic house with a revered restaurant at very reasonable prices. The tastiest lamb you'll find and particularly good scallops and halibut. ✪ *Busta, Brae • Map A1 • (01806) 522506 • £££*

STREETSMART

SCOTLAND'S TOP 10

Left **Edinburgh Festival performer** Centre **Ordnance Survery map** Right **Shoppers in Glasgow**

Planning Your Visit

1 When to Go
Scotland is a year-round destination, with continuous natural attractions, events and festivals. But outside the main Easter–Oct season, many sights, such as historic houses, either close or operate reduced opening hours. Surprisingly, the weather rarely causes disruptions to transport, but it is unpredictable even at the best of times.

2 Scotland's Weather
A maritime position ensures Scotland's highly variable weather pattern. The east is drier than the west, but rain can occur throughout the year, and heavy snowfalls are possible in winter – seldom lasting longer than a few days, except in the hills. Average summer temperatures are 15–22°C (59–72°F); average winter temperatures 1–7°C (34–45°F).

3 For How Long?
It may look small on the map, but that can be deceptive. Though only 275 miles (440 km) long, Scotland is endowed with 6,200 miles (10,000 km) of coastline and has 787 major islands. So ... allow as long as you can spare.

4 Immigration Laws
As with the rest of the UK, a valid passport is required to be shown on entry. Visitors from the European Union (EU), United States and Canada, Australia and New Zealand do not require visas, nor inoculations. Other nationals should check current regulations.

5 Opening Hours
Most shops are open 9am–5:30pm Mon–Sat. City shops usually have one late-night shopping (often until 8pm Thu) and many are now open Sun, too. Town shops often close 1pm Sat and may take an afternoon off during the week.

6 High Seasons and Holidays
What defines the "high season" (when demand and prices are at their highest) varies, but generally there are three key periods: Hogmanay (New Year), Easter and Jul–Aug. The main holidays in Scotland are 1–2 Jan, Good Friday (end Mar–early Apr), first and last Mon in May, first Mon in Aug, and 25–26 Dec.

7 Electricity and Sockets
Voltage is 220/240v 50Hz. Most places use three square-pin sockets with 3-, 5- or 13-amp fuses. Buy an adaptor at your departure airport, but check the voltage requirements of your appliances first. Most hotel bathrooms have two-pronged sockets for shavers.

8 Books and Maps
For some background reading try Magnus Magnusson's *Scotland – The Story of a Nation*, June Skinner Sawyers' *The Road North*, and Alastair Scott's humorous travels, *Native Stranger*. For guidance on the ground, many maps of Scotland are produced, some showing tourist attractions. These are useful, but the best maps for walkers are the Ordnance Survey Landranger (1:50,000) and Explorer (1:25,000) series. They are widely available throughout Scotland and are essential for any serious walking.

9 What to Pack
An umbrella, warm clothes (even heavier ones for winter) and a waterproof jacket or coat. The older, established restaurants may require men to wear a jacket and tie, but this is becoming less prevalent. Also, check out the *Getting Around Scotland* section (*see p135*) for special tickets that must be purchased before you enter the UK.

10 Smoking
Although smoking is banned in many public places, such as cinemas and theatres, some restaurants still have smoking sections. Cigarettes maintain a strong hold over a large section of Scotland's population, and pubs remain cherished dens for smokers. In city bars, expect to contend with a thick nicotine fog.

Left **Visit Scotland logo** Centre **The Scotsman newspaper** Right **Taste of Scotland**

Sources of Information

1 Visit Scotland
Visit Scotland is the renamed Scottish Tourist Board. It promotes Scotland as a visitor destination, provides good general information, publishes brochures and has a website – an excellent place to start planning your trip.

2 British Tourist Authority
The BTA operates information offices in many cities around the world. Check their internet site (see Directory box) or the British Embassy in your capital city.

3 Regional Tourist Information
Scotland has no shortage of regional tourist information offices. Most regions have several main offices open all year round, as well as smaller offices open during the summer months. These are listed throughout this guide.

4 Historic Scotland
Many of Scotland's oldest buildings are under the custodianship of this organization. If you intend visiting several it may be cheaper to become a member or buy a 3-day Scottish Explorer ticket.

5 National Trust for Scotland
This is the other large organization that cares for Scotland's exceptional buildings – mainly stately homes and castles. By buying a 3-, 7- or 14-day Discovery Ticket (individual or family), you are allowed entry to as many NTS properties as you can visit in the time.

6 Activity Holidays
Scotland is a breath of fresh air for the outdoor person. Skiing, cycling, riding, walking, sailing and watersports all have specialist organizations promoting their sports and providing advice on how visitors can best enjoy them.

7 Taste of Scotland
For epicureans, Taste of Scotland is an organization that samples all kinds of places and lists those of a good or high standard, though its listing is not comprehensive. The ToS also publicizes food festivals and events.

8 Bird and Wildlife Organizations
The Scottish Wildlife Trust operates several sanctuaries equipped with hides, and Scottish Natural Heritage manages sites of environmental interest and special habitats. The Royal Society for the Protection of Birds also has reserves across Scotland.

9 Car Breakdown Services
Although there are several smaller breakdown services, the main two are the AA (Automobile Association) and the RAC (Royal Automobile Club). Rental cars usually include free breakdown cover.

10 Local Sources
In Britain, visitor attractions are posted on brown road signs with white letters. Also check village notice boards and local newspapers for forthcoming events.

Directory

Visit Scotland
(0131) 332 2433 • www.visitscotland.com

British Tourist Authority
www.visitbritain.com

Historic Scotland
(0131) 668 8800 • www.historic-scotland.net

National Trust for Scotland
(0131) 243 9300 • www.nts.org.uk

Activity Holidays
www.activity-scotland.co.uk

Taste of Scotland
(0131) 220 1900 • www.taste-of-scotland.com

Scottish Wildlife Trust
www.swt.org.uk

Royal Society for the Protection of Birds
www.rspb.org.uk

Scottish Natural Heritage
www.snh.org.uk

Road Information
www.theaa.com
www.rac.co.uk

Taste of Scotland's annual guide, Best Tastes in Scotland, *is available in all good bookshops*

Left **Glasgow International Airport** Centre **InterCity train** Right **M8 motorway, Glasgow**

TOP 10 Getting to Scotland

1 International Airports and Connections

Scotland has four international airports: Edinburgh, 7 miles from city centre (coaches every 8–20 mins, taxis approx £15); Glasgow, 8 miles from city centre (coaches every 15–30 mins, taxis approx £12); Prestwick, 30 miles from Glasgow city centre (trains every 30 mins, coaches every hour, taxi approx £45); Aberdeen, 7 miles from city centre (coaches at peak times, taxis approx £10).

2 By Air from North America

Air Canada, Continental and American Airlines fly direct to Scotland. Other transatlantic airlines fly to London, where connecting flights are plentiful.

3 By Air from Europe

Direct flights into Scotland operate from many European cities, including Amsterdam, Copenhagen, Brussels, Frankfurt, Paris, Madrid and Dublin.

4 By Air from within the UK

Eight airlines provide regular services from cities in the UK. By far the greatest frequency of flights is out of London Heathrow and Gatwick. However, airlines other than British Airways and bmi usually depart from Stansted, Luton or London City Airport.

5 By Ferry

A new superfast ferry from Zeebrugge to Rosyth (Edinburgh) sails daily and takes 16 hrs. There are summer services from Iceland and Norway to Lerwick, and several companies provide year-round daily links to Scotland from Belfast.

6 By Train

Eurostar is the high-speed passenger rail service operating from European cities to London. From here there are frequent trains to Edinburgh (4 hrs) and Glasgow (5 hrs).

7 By Coach

Day and night services operate out of London and other major UK cities. Reliable and much cheaper than trains (some fantastic deals if you plan ahead), but journeys are longer and comfort more restricted.

8 Coach and Rail Termini

Edinburgh and Glasgow's principal train stations are Waverley and Central respectively. Both are in the middle of town. Edinburgh's main coach station is on St Andrew's Square in the New Town; Glasgow's is opposite the Royal Concert Hall at the east end of Sauchiehall St.

9 By Car

The M6, A68 and, partially coastal, A1 are the main road routes into Scotland, the latter two for Edinburgh, the former for Glasgow. No border controls, just a "Welcome to Scotland" sign.

10 Internet Bargains

Many airlines and transport companies now undercut their agents by selling cheaper tickets directly through their websites. If you can plan well ahead and be flexible about dates, you get the best deals, but last-minute bargains are also possible.

Directory

Airports
• Edinburgh (0131) 333 1000 • Glasgow (0141) 887 1111 • Prestwick (01292) 479 822 • Aberdeen (01224) 722 331

Airlines
www.continental.com
www.aa.com
www.aircanada.com
www.britishairways.com
www.easyjet.com
www.flybmi.com
www.ryanair.com
www.scotairways.co.uk

Ferries
www.superfastscot land.com • www.stena line.com • www.poirish sea.com • www.sea cat.co.uk

Trains
National Rail Enquiries: 0845 748 4950
GNER: 08457 225 225

Coaches
www.gobycoach.com
• www.citylink.co.uk

Left **Car ferry** Centre **Rural main road** Right **Edinburgh taxi**

Getting Around Scotland

1 By Air
Scotland has an excellent internal air network connecting regional airports and the islands with the main airports of Aberdeen, Edinburgh, Glasgow and Inverness. British Regional Airlines offer a Highland Rover Pass: five flights within the Highlands. Buy it at least 7 days before you arrive in the UK; contact British Airways for details.

2 By Train
Britrail offers several types of rover ticket, all of which must be bought before you get to the UK. Scotrail issue several rover tickets for sale in the UK, some of which allow access to ferries as well.

3 By Bus
Many local bus services operate but Scottish Citylink is the largest provider, serving over 200 towns and cities. City buses don't give change and their Day Tickets are cheaper after 9:30am.

4 Coach and Mini-Bus Tours
Plenty of companies offer tours of various durations and standards of accommodation. Two renowned minibus-and-hostel tour companies are Rabbie's Trail Burners and MacBackpackers.

5 Ferries
Caledonian MacBrayne is the largest ferry company and works the majority of west coast routes, but smaller companies also run ferries to and around Scotland's 130 inhabited islands.

6 Car
Roads vary from single tracks to motorways and are generally of a high standard. There are no tolls except on the Forth, Tay, Erskine and Skye bridges. *The Highway Code* details all the regulations and can be purchased in bookshops.

7 Taxis
Taxis are regulated and legally obliged to display a licence number. City taxis should be metered but in remote areas unmetered cars operate – ask for the fare before you get in.

8 Cycling
There are some great long distance and city cycle networks. Unfortunately, provisions for bike transport on trains is dire – book well in advance to reserve some of the limited space.

9 On Foot
With over a dozen major walking routes and thousands of marked footpaths, Scotland is a great place for the foot traveller. Scotland's access laws are much more lenient than England's, and walkers who do not cause damage or interfere with privacy or estate activities are generally allowed to wander the land freely.

10 Passing Places
Single-track roads have passing places to allow faster traffic behind you to overtake, and to allow two cars travelling in opposite directions to get past each other. When two cars meet between passing places, the car nearest to it should reverse and (keeping to the left) pull into, or stop opposite, the passing place.

Directory

Rail
www.britrail.net
www.scotrail.co.uk

Buses
www.citylink.co.uk

Coach tours
• *www.nithsdalecoach tours.co.uk* • *www.tour ofscotland.com* • *www. rabbies.com* • *www.mac backpackers.com*

Ferries
• *www.calmac.co.uk (Caledonian MacBrayne)*
• *www.westernferries clyde.co.uk* • *www. northlinkferries.co.uk*
• *www.orkneyferries.com*
• *www.visitshetland.com*

Cycling
• *www.sustrans.org.uk*
• *www.northsea-cycle. com*

Walking
• *www.walkaboutscot land.com* • *www. walkingwild.com*

Left **Early closing** Centre **Mist rolling in** Right **Thistle, the flower of Scotland**

ᵀᴼᴾ10 Things to Avoid

1 Traffic Snarls
Congestion around Edinburgh, Glasgow and the Forth Road Bridge is becoming a daily occurrence. Into-city queues build up from 7:30 to 9am and out-of-city from 4:30 to 6pm. If you can, avoid these areas during the rush hours. Radio Scotland (810 MW/92–94 FM) issues frequent road reports at peak periods.

2 Football Match Crowds
Not a serious problem for visitors as football is not a summer sport and fans are usually well behaved. However, they can be boisterous and noisy, and cause traffic congestion.

3 Midges
These minute flies, which come in clouds and cause itching bites, are the curse of the west coast. They love warm, windless evenings and boggy terrain. From the end of May to mid-Sep they can pop up to ruin an al fresco evening. Dozens of repellents are available, but the wonder cure has yet to appear. Midge nets are essential for campers.

4 Early Closings
In remoter parts of Scotland and particularly on the islands, the volume of trade does not justify long opening hours, so it's easy to be caught out. Don't assume that shops or

restaurants will be open late. And in the Western Isles in particular, Sunday is still predominantly a day of rest (see p59).

5 "Sorry, it's fully booked …"
Accommodation in Edinburgh for the August festivals gets booked up months in advance. This is the most extreme case but you should reserve beds and tickets for main events in advance of any festival in Scotland, and also car space on ferries during peak periods.

6 Unexpected Weather
Scotland's northern latitude and unpredictable weather pattern mean that conditions can alter rapidly. Winter weather in the hills can be particularly severe and apt to change with very little warning. Avoid getting caught out by taking sufficient clothes for the worst the season could throw at you, and listen to weather forecasts, which are updated regularly on radio stations.

7 The Stalking Season
The controlled cull of Scotland's over-population of red deer is an essential aspect of estate and countryside management, besides being an important source of income. The main "Stalking Season", as it's called, runs from mid-

August to 20 October. During this period, or wherever signs are posted, walkers are requested to seek permission from estate owners before they take to the hills.

8 Car Break-ins and Lost Possessions
Although theft from cars is not common, it does occur. To reduce the risk, avoid leaving valuables on display when you leave your car. If you lose anything, contact the nearest police station to see if it has been handed in – it does happen!

9 Traffic Accidents
If you come to Scotland from a country that drives on the right, confusion over the direction in which to look for on-coming traffic can easily catch you out. Use pedestrian crossings wherever possible, and, if driving, take particular care when rejoining a road after a break and when approaching road junctions, especially roundabouts.

10 Calling a Thistle a Rose
The Scots are somewhat touchy on the subject of national pride, and for good reason (see pp32–3). Take care not to refer to Britain as "England" or – even worse – to Scotland as "England". The latter is a guaranteed conversation-stopper.

Left **Police car** Centre **Pharmacy** Right **Mountain stream**

🔟 Health and Security

1 Emergencies
For any emergency, there's just one number to dial: 999. This covers police, ambulance, fire brigade, coastguard and mountain rescue. You will receive immediate attention and be asked which service you require.

2 Hospitals
All hospitals operate an Accident and Emergency department where you can receive treatment on a priority system. You can rely on attention for accidents and emergencies at a hospital, but for any other ailment you should consult a doctor.

3 Doctors and Dentists
Doctors and dentists are listed in the *Yellow Pages* (phonebook), or you can consult a tourist information office. Doctors usually have certain consulting hours when people can come and wait to be seen. Dentists rarely have unfilled appointments, but will always try to fit in an emergency.

4 Medical Charges
Emergency medical care is free but additional treatment may incur charges. Doctors' consultations are free for visitors whose home country has reciprocal health arrangements with the UK, but drugs must be paid for at a standard charge. Documentation will be required. Other visitors will be charged as private patients and must pay the full cost of any medication prescribed.

5 Chemists
Chemists (pharmacists) sell a wide range of medicines that are available without a prescription. In most cities at least one chemist stays open until midnight. If you depend on certain medication, it's best to bring a supply with you. Ask your doctor to write out the generic name (rather than the brand name) to help locate its equivalent over here.

6 Water
Tap water is safe to drink in Scotland and so, thank goodness, is the water from hill burns (streams) – useful if you're out walking all day. It might be rash to say that there is never any danger, so if in doubt check with locals. Scotland also has plenty of fine spring and mineral water in bottles.

7 Crime
Scotland is not a dangerous country, but assaults and muggings do take place in the larger towns and cities. Take the same precautions that you would in any city: avoid deserted and unlit places, use your intuition about entering less salubrious areas and don't flaunt money, jewellery or other coveted valuables.

8 Pickpockets
Again, not common, but they are about. Be especially wary in crowds. Avoid keeping your wallet in a back (or any loose) pocket, and only carry about your "day money". Keep a separate record of credit card numbers and the action to take if they go missing.

9 Road Reports
In addition to the information under Traffic Snarls *(see p136)*, the AA operates a Road Watch scheme which lists all problems on the roads (calls cost 50p per minute). Call them if you're worried about your route; especially useful if there's the prospect of frost or snow.

10 Car Safety
The wearing of seat belts is compulsory for all car travellers (front and back), and the police can fine anyone not doing so. It is illegal to eat, drink or use a mobile phone while in control of a moving vehicle. Do not drive after drinking alcohol. The tolerated limit is low, and the penalty for exceeding it is severe.

Directory

Traffic Reports
AA Road Watch: 09003 401 100

Weather Information
www.metoffice.com
www.scotlandonline.com

Left **Port-na-Con, child-friendly (see p149)** Centre **Disabled access** Right **Hertz car hire sign**

🔟 Families, Groups & Special Needs

1 Family Discounts
Discount tickets for families are available on trains and buses, and for visiting properties under the care of the National Trust for Scotland and Historic Scotland *(see Sources of Information, p133)*. Ask at other visitor attractions – most will offer some discount.

2 Children-Friendly Accommodation
Not all guesthouses or B&Bs cater for children. It's worth asking at tourist information offices for those that do, or asking proprietors when making reservations. Children-friendly establishments tend to have family rooms or advertise safe gardens or play areas.

3 Family Rooms
Regional accommodation guides will indicate if an establishment offers family rooms. Many hostels also offer family rooms, but these are usually limited and you should book well in advance.

4 Self-Catering
Aside from camping and hostelling, this is probably the cheapest family and group accommodation you can find. It does restrict you to one place for a week (usually the minimum rental period) but having a base from which to make trips can be just the ticket. Regional accommodation guides list self-catering cottages and caravans but there are also many independent letting agencies *(see pp143 & 145)*.

5 Disabled Access
Visit Scotland issues a fact sheet listing all establishments that cater for those with mobility difficulties. Visitor attractions vary in their provision for disabled access: modern sights tend to be good but historic buildings may not be suitable for wheelchairs – contact them in advance.

6 Capability Scotland
This is Scotland's largest disability organization. It provides a national advice and information service and is extremely helpful. It can, for example, supply information on where and when Shopmobility facilities are available.

7 Holiday Care Service
Based in London, this is a national charity and the UK's central source of holiday and travel information for disabled people and their carers.

8 RADAR
Another London-based organization, which provides general information for disabled travellers.

9 Seagull Trust
A small charity, with canal boats on the Forth (Edinburgh) and Caledonian (Inverness) canals specifically designed for disabled people to take to the water. Their programme is mainly for local groups but with adequate notice they may have room for visitors.

10 Hand-Controlled Rental Cars
Hertz Rent A Car can supply hand-controlled vehicles at no extra cost but these should be ordered in advance. Special Disabled Parking bays and free access (such as a toll-free crossing of the Skye Bridge) are available but you must display an official sign in your car. The AA Disability Helpline can advise on many aspects of road use for the disabled.

Directory

Visit Scotland Information
(0131) 332 2433

Capability Scotland
• *www.capability-scotland.org.uk*
• *(0131) 313 5510*

Holiday Care
• *www.holidaycare.org.uk* • *(01293) 774 535*

RADAR
• *www.radar.org.uk*
• *(020) 7250 3222*

The Seagull Trust
(0131) 229 1789

AA Disability Helpline
0800 262050

Free regional accommodation guides are available from local tourist offices – look out for the Visit Scotland logo (see p133)

Left **Tartan clothing** Centre **Whisky Shop, Edinburgh** Right **Edinburgh Crystal**

Shopping Tips

1 VAT Refunds
Value Added Tax (VAT) at 17.5% is applied to goods and services. Non-EU visitors can reclaim VAT on goods only by using the Foreign Exchange Tax-Free Shopping form at participating stores; you'll need to show your passport. This form is presented at Customs on leaving the UK.

2 Prices and Bargains
Britain is not particularly cheap for shopping, but prices can vary considerably, so it pays to shop around. End of season sales offer the best bargains, as can outdoor markets, but beware of inferior products.

3 Scottish Made
In a global economy where shops can be swamped with imported "Scottish" souvenirs, it's refreshing to find some outlets that specialize in quality home-produced arts and crafts. Two such shops are Made In Scotland (Beauly) and Highland Origins in Dornie.

4 Kilts, Tartans and Tweed
Scotland's tartans (see p58) come in hundreds of patterns and dozens of forms, notably the kilt. These are complex garments to make and require several weeks' work. Tweed for suits, jackets and skirts also comes in a wide array of designs.

5 Woollens
Shetland and Arran are the two best-known sources of woollens, but it would be wrong to restrict your search, as woollen and cashmere design has excelled in the last two decades. For beautiful and unusual wear, try Ragamuffin (12a St Mary's St, Edinburgh).

6 Packaged Food
Packaged food can make excellent presents to take home. Smoked salmon, kippers (smoked herring), haggis (see p65), Dundee cake and shortbread are all popular souvenirs of Scotland.

7 Drinks
You could take home Moniack wines or Drambuie liqueur, but by far the most popular drink is whisky, in standard bottles, miniatures or special presentation cartons. Sadly, it's highly taxed and often cheaper outside the UK.

8 Jewellery
Another flourishing area of innovative design. It seems that dozens of new and talented silversmiths set up shop each year. Orkney produces an astonishing array of quality jewellery. Some of the more popular traditional designs feature Celtic knotwork and other interwoven patterns, and make use of the Cairngorm, an orange semi-precious stone.

9 Glass
Two regions are famed for their glassware. Caithness Glass (see p125) is a world leader in the production of exquisitely designed and crafted paperweights, while Edinburgh Glass specializes in beautifully engraved goblets, whisky and wine decanters and drinking vessels.

10 Art Works
Galleries selling art can be found all over Scotland. Here are three in Scotland's major cities: Edinburgh Printmakers deal in contemporary fine art printmaking. Stills (also Edinburgh) is a long-established gallery, and Street Level (Glasgow) specializes in "dynamic photographic culture".

Directory

Made in Scotland
www.made-in-scotland.co.uk

Highland Origins
www.highlandorigins.com

Other Useful Sites
• www.touristpublications.co.uk/edin/edinshop.htm
• www.ortak.co.uk
• www.caithnessglass.co.uk • www.edinburgh-crystal.co.uk
• www.edinburgh-printmakers.co.uk
• www.stills.org
• www.sl-photoworks.demon.co.uk

Left **High street bank** Centre **Clydesdale Bank logo** Right **Student card**

Banking and Communications

1 Currency
Britain's currency is the pound sterling (£), divided into 100 pence (p). Scotland's three banks each produce different-faced notes but these, along with Bank of England and Northern Ireland notes, are all legal tender throughout the UK. Scottish notes come in £1, £5, £10, £20, £50 and £100 denominations. Coins come as 1p, 2p, 5p, 10p, 20p, 50p, £1 and £2.

2 Changing Money
Banks tend to offer the best exchange rates and are open 9am–5pm Mon–Fri. In remote areas you may find a mobile bank parked and open for business. Bureaux de Change work longer hours in the main cities and at airports but their commission charges can be high.

3 ATMs
ATMs, or "holes-in-the-wall" as they are affectionately called, can be found widely throughout the country, even in the Highlands and islands. Also, most supermarkets offer a cashback service when you purchase provisions with a debit card carrying the Switch or Cirrus logo.

4 Credit Cards
Credit cards are widely accepted across Scotland but many small shops, cafés and most B&Bs deal only in cash or cheques in sterling. VISA and Mastercard are the most commonly presented cards. Certain outlets also accept Diners Club and American Express.

5 Traveller's Cheques
Traveller's cheques are still the safest means of carrying money and, if in pounds sterling, you can use them directly to pay for goods and services. Check on commission charges when purchasing or cashing your cheques, as practices vary. Keep your receipts separate from the cheques as you will need them in the event of loss or theft.

6 Internet Access
Internet cafés are relatively common in the cities. EasyEverything has 400-terminal cafés in the centres of both Glasgow and Edinburgh. Internet access is harder to find elsewhere, but most towns will have at least one café, or some libraries and hotels may provide this service.

7 Phone Boxes
Public phones are dotted about all over the place. Some accept credit cards, but the majority require either coins or a phonecard which can be purchased at many shops. To call an operator dial 100.

8 Mobile Phones
Coverage for mobile phones now extends across most of Scotland but there are still pockets in the Highlands and Islands outside the range of signals. Vodaphone and BT Cellnet currently have the most effective networks in Scotland.

9 Post
The mail is still regarded as an honourable and sacred institution. Mail boxes may be freestanding or set in walls, and a notice specifies the collection times. These are reliable. Post offices work normal business hours. Many shops also sell stamps. Main post offices operate a Poste Restante service and will hold mail for one month.

10 Student and Other Discounts
Most entertainment venues, visitor attractions and travel services offer discount (often termed "concessions") to students on production of an appropriate ID. Some organizations, eg the National Trust for Scotland, also offer cheaper entry to holders of Youth Hostel cards. Discounts for the elderly are sometimes available but are less common. It's always worth asking.

Internet Access

EasyEverything
• 58 Rose St, Edinburgh
• 57–61 St Vincent Street, Glasgow

Left **Coldingham Youth Hostel** Right **Camping and caravan site**

⑩ Accommodation Tips

1 Hotels
The highest standard of accommodation is to be found in hotels, but they vary greatly in facilities, quality and price. Cost generally reflects quality but you can find some great wee (small) hotels that cost little more than good B&Bs. VisitScotland produces a range of guides on all types of accommodation.

2 Guesthouses and B&Bs
There is little to distinguish guesthouses and B&Bs. They both offer rooms in private homes with breakfast included, and you are expected to be absent during the day. They offer great opportunities for meeting locals.

3 Self-Catering
Self-catering flats, cottages and caravans are the most cost-effective forms of accommodation for families and groups, aside from camping and hostels. Organizations such as Visit Scotland publish nationwide listings. See also the *Where to Stay* section for Glasgow and Edinburgh *(see pp142–5)*.

4 Discounts for Longer Stays
If you're planning on staying longer than two nights in any one place, most hotels, guesthouses and B&Bs will give discounts, as well as offering special weekly rates.

5 Reservations
Aside from the qualifications mentioned in *Things to Avoid (p136)*, you can generally tour Scotland without reservations unless you are intent on staying in a particular establishment. This also applies to Youth Hostels, which once had an open-door policy but now can be fully booked.

6 Look for Signs
Tourist accommodation guides and those of other organizations work on the basis that proprietors pay to have their establishment inspected and listed. Many smaller hotels, guesthouses and B&Bs do not consider this worthwhile, so these guides are far from comprehensive. Look out for roadside signs and, if you're stuck, ask a local.

7 Hostels
The Scottish Youth Hostel Association (SYHA) operates many excellent hostels in Scotland and publishes a brochure listing them. Take your membership card and travel with a sheet (some require a sleeping bag). Recently, hundreds of independent hostels have sprung up, and they have their own website; no membership necessary.

8 Caravaning and Camping
There's no shortage of these either and they are usually of a high standard and beautifully located. Reduced facilities may be offered in remoter areas but the prices will be lower and the views probably even better.

9 Wild Camping
Unless signposted to the contrary, wild camping is tolerated in quiet places where you do not infringe on anyone's privacy. Always try and find the landowner to ask permission first.

10 Mountain Bothies
The Mountain Bothy Association is a charity that looks after over 100 unlocked "bothies" (simple wooden, iron or stone huts). These are all in remote areas and usually have little more than a fireplace, table, seats and a sleeping platform – free but donations appreciated.

Directory

Self-Catering
• *The Society of Scotland's Self-Caterers, www.assc.co.uk/index.shtml* • *Scottish Holiday Cottages, www.scottish-holiday-cottages.co.uk*

Hostel and Camping websites
• www.syha.org.uk
• www.hostel-scotland.co.uk • www.camping-site.org.uk/grounds.htm
• www.mountain bothies.org.uk

For a selection of island retreats, including self-catering cottages, hotels and hostels, **see pp44–5**

Left **Balmoral** Centre **Meridien** Right **The Witchery's Secret Garden dining room**

Edinburgh: Luxury Hotels

1 Balmoral
The most prestigious of Edinburgh's old-school hotels, right in the heart of things on Princes St. Sports facilities and two great restaurants, Number One Princes Street and Hadrian's brasserie. ◉ *1 Princes St • Map N2–3 • (0131) 556 2414 • reservations@thebalmoral hotel.com • £££££*

2 Scotsman
Formerly home of the *Scotsman* newspaper, this solid building has been transformed into rather a stylish hotel, especially in regard to its leisure facilities, which feature a sleek, steel and granite pool. Well-appointed bedrooms, superbly situated (looking north over the New Town) and with a fine restaurant, Vermilion. ◉ *20 North Bridge St • Map P3 • (0131) 556 5565 • www.thescots manhotel.co.uk • £££££*

3 Albany
Three Georgian houses in the New Town, joined to form a smartly decked-out hotel. The Albany's restaurant, Haldanes, is one of the main draws, with a reputation for great Scottish fare. ◉ *39 Albany St • Map N1 • (0131) 556 0397 • info@albanyhotel edinburgh.co.uk • ££££*

4 Caledonian Hilton
With its very formal Pompadour restaurant and the Cally Bar for shooting the breeze with friends, the Caledonian is something of an institution, despite its new Hilton-chain status. Opulence, indulgence and great views at a price. ◉ *Princes St & Lothian Rd • Map L3 • (0131) 222 8888 • £££££*

5 Sheraton Grand
Looking rather pale and charmless on the outside, the Sheraton is nonetheless a fine hotel in terms of its facilities, especially the state-of-the-art health club. Good Italian and Scottish restaurants at hand, and in the locale of the West End business district. ◉ *Festival Sq, Lothian Rd • Map L4 • (0131) 229 9131 • £££££*

6 Channings
Wonderfully peaceful setting, away from the hubbub. Décor reflects the Edwardian architecture, while the in-room facilities are up to the minute, with internet access, DVD players and e-TV. Luxurious bathrooms, with Molton Brown toiletries. ◉ *15 Sth Learmonth Gdns • Map J1 • (0131) 315 2226 • www. channings.co.uk • ££££*

7 Meridien
Formerly the Royal Terrace, the Meridien sits above much of Edinburgh, drinking in the views from its splendid garden terrace. Regal décor, sports facilities and whirlpool baths in most bathrooms. ◉ *18 Royal Terrace • Map Q1 • (0131) 557 3222 • ££££*

8 Witchery
Champagne and chocolates await each guest in this cocoon of romance. Bose sound systems and cable TV are the modern touches to otherwise antique-filled rooms, where swathes of rich cloth run amok. Only six suites, but such decadence in Scotland must be rationed. For the restaurant, see p77. ◉ *Castlehill • Map M4 • (0131) 225 5613 • ££££*

9 The Howard
The Georgian character of the Howard extends to the service, too, and every room comes with a dedicated butler to pamper you throughout your stay. The Atholl restaurant is on site for period dining, or have a full à la carte meal served in your room – by your own butler, of course! ◉ *34 Great King St • Map M1 • (0131) 557 3500 • www. thehoward.com • £££££*

10 The Bonham
Run by the same team as The Howard and Channings, The Bonham is the most chic of the three. Confident styling, using contemporary furnishings and the full gamut of communication and entertainment devices (fast internet access, DVDs etc). The restaurant tilts towards modern European. ◉ *35 Drums-heugh Gdns • Map K3 • (0131) 623 6060 • www. thebonham.com • ££££*

Streetsmart

Left **Malmaison** Right **The Point's sleek interior**

Mid-Range and Boutique Hotels

1 Malmaison

As its name suggests, Malmaison looks to France for inspiration, and pro-vides a winning mix of good brasserie food and contemporary styling in its rooms – wonderful bathrooms! Nicely set on the quay, next to Fishers (see p77). ◈ 1 Tower Place, Leith • Map K5 • (0131) 468 5000 • www.malmaison. com • £££

2 Apex City Hotel

Joining its sister hotel up the road at No. 31, with modern, simple and functional rooms, and a mix of business and family facilities (photocopying and secretarial services in the former case, cots and high chairs in the latter). ◈ 61 Grassmarket • Map M4 • (0131) 243 3456 • £££

3 Inverleith Hotel

Victorian town house hotel, close to the glorious Botanic Garden (see p50). Try for the sump-tuous four-poster room, or consider the Georgian self-catering apartment in the New Town. ◈ 5 Inver-leith Terrace • Map K5 • (0131) 556 2745 • ££ (£££ for self-catering apartment)

4 Point

The most style-conscious hotel in town. Broad sweeps of intense colour add vitality to the sharp minimalism through-out, and the bedrooms and bathrooms are very well appointed and deeply relaxing. Good restaurant and one of the best bars in town (see p76). ◈ 34 Bread St • Map L5 • (0131) 221 5555 • www.point-hotel. co.uk • £££

5 George Inter-Continental

The George retains many period details and trades on its evocation of a bygone era – the early 19th century to be precise. Price category a little misleading, as cheaper deals can nearly always be struck. ◈ 9–21 George St • Map M2 • (0131) 225 1251 • ££££

6 Number 17

Beautifully decorated Victorian West End home, and great cooking too. Comfort is assured in the bedrooms, and breakfast is served in the ample kitchen, using Scottish fare such as potato scones and Aberdeen butteries to augment the usual fry-up staples. ◈ 17 Lear-month Terr • Map J1 • (0131) 315 4088 • ££

7 Sibbet House Apartments

Two spacious, central locations for self-catering in style. The Northumber-land St apartment offers two double rooms and a single; the leafy Aber-cromby Place property has a double, plus two beds in a screened-off section of the living room. Two/three-night booking policy. ◈ 28A Northumberland St; Map M1/2 • 26 Abercromby Pl; Map M2 • (0131) 624 0084 • www.26abercrombyplace. co.uk • ££

8 Holiday Inn Crowne Plaza

Castle-like building on the Royal Mile. Spacious, if uninspiring, bedrooms within, and a plentiful supply of facilities, from the restaurant with light-ing that recalls Watt's first electrical experiments (see p34) to the leisure club, with jet pool, sauna and solarium. ◈ 80 High St • Map P3 • (0131) 557 9797 • www.crowne plazaed.co.uk • £££

9 Rick's

Very stylish rooms, with the contemporary chic of walnut head-boards paired with angora blankets. Such tactile comforts are complemented by DVD players, modem points and very good sound systems. See also p76. ◈ 55a Frederick St • Map M2 • (0131) 622 7800 • ££

10 Ingrams

Small B&B hotel, nicely placed in the New Town – quiet and leafy, yet close to many good restaurants, plus the shops of George St, Rose St and Princes St. Smartly decorated rooms, in a 19th-century ilk, with the modern requirements of TV and drinks facilities. ◈ 24 Northumberland St • Map M1 • (0131) 556 8140 • ££

Left **St Christopher's Inn** Right **Eglinton Youth Hostel**

🔟 Edinburgh: Budget and Hostels

1 Herald House Hotel
An absolute steal – bright and comfortable modern hotel, hewn from a rustic stone building to the west of the city centre. In such a compact capital, none of the main sights is very far away, and either the Old Town or Princes St can be reached within a 15-minute walk. TVs in all the rooms, decent beds, uncluttered décor, en-suite showers. 🚇 *70 Grove St • Map K5 • (0131) 228 2323 • ££*

2 Ibis Hotel
Smart, neat, clean, functional hotel that makes up for in prime location (just off the Royal Mile) what it lacks in generosity of space in the tiny bedrooms and bathrooms. 🚇 *6 Hunter Square • Map P3 • (0131) 240 7000 • ££*

3 Borough
Pick of the budget hotels – fantastic value for a modern chic hotel. Unfussy décor and large windows give a convincing illusion of space in bedrooms that come with all the minimalist frills: that is, fancy TV, DVD player and full-on waterfall-type shower in the bathroom. 🚇 *72 Causewayside • Map P6 • (0131) 668 2255 • ££*

4 Raeburn House
Located in the residential area of Stockbridge – about a 10-minute walk from Princes St – Raeburn House is a fine Georgian villa. Pleasant décor with understated floral patterns and plenty of space. Currently, none of the rooms offers en-suite facilities (hence the budget price tag), but the hotel is to be upgraded in 2003. Festival Inns, who own the Raeburn, have various other hotels around town. 🚇 *112 Raeburn Place • Map K1 • (0131) 622 6800 • £*

5 Jury's Edinburgh Inn
Rising up above Waverley Station, and therefore enjoying splendid views, this is one of the smarter budget chain hotels. Décor is kept simple, and all the rooms have satellite TV and air-conditioning – on the off chance that the city's temparature soars. Well placed for the Old Town attractions, and a short walk over North Bridge to Princes St. 🚇 *43 Jeffrey St • Map P3 • (0131) 200 3300 • ££*

6 St Christopher's Inn Hostel
A new style of hostel that provides a mix of dormitory and private rooms, some en suite. As well as laundry facilities and lockers, there are hot tubs, saunas and internet access. There's also a bar on site. 🚇 *9–13 Market St • Map N3 • (0131) 226 1446 • £*

7 Eglinton Youth Hostel
Unlike most of the other hostels in Edinburgh, this one is away from the madding crowd, amid the genteel respectability of the West End, though still within a 10-minute walk of Princes St. Lounge areas, games room, kitchen and laundry; dormitory accommodation only. 🚇 *18 Eglinton Cres • Map J4 • (0131) 337 1120 • £*

8 Brodies Backpackers Hostel
One of the smaller hostels, and all the more cosy and relaxed for that. Room for 56 guests in spacious dorms with white stone walls and wooden floors. Good showers, laundry and cooking facilities, and – as with all the hostels, in fact – superbly located, in this case right in the thick of it on the Royal Mile. 🚇 *12 High Street • Map P3 • (0131) 556 6770 • £*

9 High Street Hostel
Bustling 24-hour hostel, central to the action. No frills, but plenty of smiling faces, most off to spend money saved on accommodation in the local bars. 🚇 *8 Blackfriars St • Map P3 • (0131) 557 3984 • £*

10 Backpackers, Royal Mile
The smallest of the hostels, with room for 38 in simple, clean dormitories. Backpackers also has the Castle Rock hostel (0131 225 9666) if other branches are full. 🚇 *105 High St • Map P3 • (0131) 557 6120 • £*

Price Categories

For a standard, double room per night (with breakfast if included), taxes and extra charges.

£	under £50
££	£50–100
£££	£100–150
££££	£150–200
£££££	over £200

St Jude's

TOP 10 Glasgow: Luxury Hotels

1 One Devonshire Gardens

This stretch of Victorian terrace in the West End is the epitome of timeless, sophisticated luxury. The rooms, individually styled, are awash with luxurious fabrics to excite the touch and selected antique furniture. With sumptuous bathrooms and one of the best restaurants in Scotland *(see p64)*, would you bother to step outside the front door? 🕾 *1 Devonshire Gdns, off Gt Western Rd • (0141) 339 2001 • £££££*

2 Arthouse Hotel

Extravagant (almost) to the point of kitsch, this velvet-clad, gold-trimmed hotel is in the funky Philippe Starck mould. The rooms are spacious, with big beds and pillows you could nest in. The sense of luxury is continued in the ample bathrooms. 🕾 *129 Bath St • Map S2 • (0141) 221 6789 • £££*

3 Glasgow Hilton

Big and modern, the Hilton has Glasgow's fullest range of facilities, including gym, pool, beauty salon, business utilities, baby-sitting and two good restaurants. Superbly appointed rooms, some with cityscape views. 🕾 *1 William St, off Pitt St • Map S2 • (0141) 204 5555 • £££££*

4 Hilton Glasgow Grosvenor

Not quite as many amenities as the central Hilton *(above)*, but a finer building (an elegant Victorian terrace) and location – in Glasgow's leafy West End, opposite the Botanic Gardens. A traditional ambience, and bedrooms every bit as comfy as its downtown sister's. 🕾 *Great Western Rd • Map V1 • (0141) 339 8811 • ££££*

5 St Jude's

A small hotel with a private-club feel, its rooms (small oases of serenity in a cool, contemporary style) situated above the restaurant and wonderful bar *(see p95)*. St Jude may be the patron of lost souls, but this style-conscious headquarters of hedonism is no place for the downhearted. 🕾 *190 Bath St • Map S2 • (0141) 352 8800 • ££*

6 Malmaison

Malmaison *(see also p143)* exercises its mantra of getting the details right: large, comfortable beds, mood lighting and seriously pleasurable bathrooms, with power showers and baths suitable for hour-long soaks. French-style brasserie in the crypt (the building is a converted church) and a gym to counterbalance all the lazing about. 🕾 *278 West George St • Map S2 • (0141) 572 1000 • £££*

7 Langs

Crisp, no-nonsense, well-designed rooms, kitted out with the usual gadgets – TV, DVD player and music system – but the real star is the Japanese-influenced Oshi spa, which chimes with the sushi restaurant. 🕾 *Port Dundas Place • Map T2 • (0141) 333 1500 • ££*

8 Millennium Hotel Glasgow

One of the best things about this large, recently revamped hotel is the conservatory, which sits on the edge of George Sq. Breakfast here, and watch the crowds rushing to and from the neighbouring station. Elsewhere, solid, dependable rooms and services, if a bit corporate in style. 🕾 *George Square • Map U2 • (0141) 332 6711 • £££*

9 Dreamhouse Inc

An excellent choice if you're staying for more than a few nights. Luxurious apartments, elegant modern styling and full maid service. Various West End locations near to Kelvingrove Park. One and two beds available, from one night to a month or more. 🕾 *Dreamhouse Inc • (0141) 332 3620 • www.dreamapartments. co.uk • £££*

10 SACO

Twelve luxury-on-a-budget one-bedroom apartments in the heart of town. Simple, modern furnishings and fully serviced: minimum 6 nights' stay. 🕾 *53 Cochrane St • Map U3 • (0117) 970 6999 • www.saco apartments.co.uk • ££*

Left **Babbity Bowster sign** Centre **Willow Hotel** Right **Baird Hall**

Streetsmart

🔟 Glasgow: Mid-Range and Budget

1 The Brunswick
A smart, copper-topped building in the buzzing Merchant City area. A modern-chic interior that's not too formal, and a delightful penthouse apartment, which can sleep six – all can squeeze into the sauna, too. ✆ 106–108 Brunswick St • Map U3 • (0141) 552 0001 • ££

2 Cathedral House
An impressively turreted Neo-Gothic red-brick house, formerly the administrative quarters for the nearby Cathedral, which some rooms over-look.The restaurant serves rather good Scottish cuisine. Very atmospheric, aided by the presence of two live-in ghosts. ✆ 28–32 Cathedral Sq • Map V3 • (0141) 552 3519 • ££–£££

3 Babbity Bowster
Named after an 18th-century wedding dance, this inn was built around 1790 and maintains a traditional style. The rooms sit above the popular and convivial bar and restaurant (see p95) and offer fittingly simple, yet comfortable lodgings. ✆ 16–18 Blackfriars La • Map U3 • (0141) 552 5055 • ££

4 Bewleys
Behind its curiously angular (and, frankly, gob-smackingly ugly) glass façade, Bewleys offers superb value for money. Very central location, and spacious rooms with pristine facilities and pretty good styling. All have TVs and modem points. ✆ 110 Bath St • Map T2 • (0141) 353 0800 • ££

5 Merchant Lodge
The former home of Glasgow's tobacco merchants, the house has been renovated to provide 40 individually styled rooms (so choose with care), all with shiny pine floors. Owned by the McMillan group, who also have the Townhouse Hotel, near Kelvingrove Park, and the Victorian House, near Glasgow School of Art. ✆ 52 Virginia St • Map U3 • (0141) 552 2424 • ££

6 Novotel
While the Novotel is unlikely to feed the mind with recollections of a truly memorable stay, it does the job of providing simple, comfortable accommodation with inoffensive décor, and food and drink readily at hand in the pleasant bar/restaurant. ✆ 181 Pitt St • Map S2 • (0141) 222 2775 • ££

7 Willow Hotel
Renfrew Street is lined by small, B&B-type hotels, and the Willow, along with the Victorian House (see Merchant Lodge entry), are the best of them. All have a certain old-fashioned charm, but the Willow has a little more spruce-ness about it. Simply adorned rooms, and well located for a stroll down the hill into town. ✆ Renfrew St • Map S1 • (0141) 332 2332 • £

8 Ibis Hotel
Like its neighbour, Novotel, Ibis isn't a prospect to get the heart racing, but it does provide even better value, achieved through an even tighter economy of scale in the bedrooms and, particularly, the bathrooms. Central location, and as a place to take a shower and curl up for the night, drifting off to late-night TV, it's hard to beat for price. ✆ West Regent St • Map S2 • (0141) 225 6000 • £

9 Glasgow Backpackers Hostel
Superbly sited hostel, high up on the fringes of Kelvingrove Park. Small dorms for the most part, plus the odd twin room; separate bathrooms. The SYHA hostel is just a few doors along. ✆ 17 Park Terrace • Map V1 • (0141) 332 9099 • Closed in winter • No credit cards • £

🔟 Baird Hall
Hostel-type accommodation in the University of Strathclyde's Art Deco hall of residence. An air of neglected magnificence abounds, so for the stylistically curious, not the faint-hearted. To continue the Deco theme, pop over the road to the moody Variety bar. ✆ 460 Sauchiehall St • Map S2 • (0141) 553 4148 • No credit cards • £

Note: Unless otherwise stated all hotels accept credit cards and have en-suite bathrooms

Price Categories

For a standard, double room per night (with breakfast if included), taxes and extra charges.

£	under £50
££	£50–100
£££	£100–150
££££	£150–200
£££££	over £200

Left **Isle of Eriska Hotel** Right **Boath House**

🔟 Country House Hotels

1 Isle of Eriska Hotel, Ledaig

Extravagant luxury on an island sanctuary near the mouth of Loch Linnhe. This should be the definition of good living *(see p44)*. 🚫 Map E3 • (01631) 720371 • www.eriska-hotel.co.uk • £££££

2 Boath House, Moray

A Georgian mansion set amid gardens and woodland, this is not just a hotel but also a retreat. Sauna, spa, gym and a full range of beauty treatments, including Ayurvedic remedies. Good healthy food, too. 🚫 Auldearn, Nairn • Map D4 • (01667) 454896 • www.boath-house.com • £££

3 Flodigarry Country House, Skye

Close to the sea and below the Trotternish Ridge stands this 19th-century mansion, which retains many period features, including a magnificent billiard room. Marvellous views from the sunny conservatory. Affordable retreat with a glowing reputation for good food. 🚫 Staffin, Isle of Skye • Map C2 • (01470) 552203 • www.flodigarry.co.uk • £££

4 Cameron House, Loch Lomond

An enduring favourite to which many stars hop by helicopter from Glasgow. Right on Loch Lomond, this turreted mansion has extensive leisure facilities, including a large pool, tennis courts and a marina. Three AA-rosette dining room, plus an all-day brasserie. 🚫 Nr Luss • Map F4 • (01389) 755565 • £££££

5 Tomdoun Hotel, Glengarry

A fine old Victorian sporting lodge that offers convivial hospitality. B&B only, or join all the guests around a table for dinner. A host of munroes to climb nearby, and fishing and stalking arranged. Warm fires and drying room. 🚫 Nr Invergarry • Map D3 • (01809) 511218 • www.tomdoun-sporting-lodge.com • ££

6 Jedforest Country Hotel, Jedburgh

Comfortable without being luxurious, this is an ideal treat for a family watching their budget. With fully-equipped rooms and its award-winning Bardoulets Restaurant, this hotel rests in spacious grounds with spots for fishing. 🚫 Camptown, Jedburgh • Map G6 • (01835) 840222 • www.jedforesthotel.free serve.co.uk • ££

7 Busta House Hotel, Shetland

Remote and peaceful, this is one of the great get-away-from-it-all retreats. First-class in every respect and detail *(see p45)*. 🚫 Brae • Map A1 • (01806) 522506 • www.busta house.com • ££££

8 Fauhope, Melrose

Built in 1897, this secluded house has enchanting views to the River Tweed and Eildon Hills. Tastefully decorated and impeccable hospitality. The food is excellent as Fauhope is run by Sheila Robson, restaurateur of Marmions *(see p83)*. For comfort and price, this ranks among the best in the Borders. 🚫 Gattonside, Melrose • Map G5 • (01896) 823184 • ££

9 Glen Clova Hotel, Glen Clova

Recently refurbished and plumped up with feathers, this excellent old hotel offers character and relaxation in the best of central Scotland's scenery. From a bunkhouse to a four-poster bed, and bar snacks to cordon bleu, this place offers beds and food for all needs. 🚫 Nr Kirriemuir, • Map E5 • (01575) 550350 • www.clova.com • £££

10 Kinnaird, Dunkeld

At the top end of the market, this ivy-clad mansion is enveloped in its own estate, through which the gamekeeper will take you on a personal tour. From the embroidered "K" on the linen to the teddy on the bed, everything is perfectly set. Food à la mode by a multi-prize-winning chef. 🚫 Map E5 • (01796) 482440 • www.kinnairdestate.com • £££££

Left **Inverlochy Castle** Centre **Kildrummy Castle Hotel** Right **Culloden House**

TOP10 Historic Houses and Castles

1 Skibo Castle, Dornoch

Madonna and Bill Clinton stay here, and if £800 per day fazes you, don't read on. Scotland's most expensive hotel is in fact a club: you may stay once, after that you must join in order to re-acquaint yourself with the luxurious surrounds. Golf galore, unbelievable quality and, of course, very discreet. ❧ Map C4 • (01862) 894600 • £££££ plus

2 Inverlochy Castle, Fort William

So long among Scotland's elite it has become the yardstick for excellence. Sumptuous décor, falconry displays on the lawn and a surrounding mountain landscape. The King of Norway presented the dining room furniture, and he wouldn't be disappointed with what's served upon it. ❧ Torlundy, Fort William • Map E3 • (01397) 702177 • www.inverlochy. co.uk • £££££

3 Kildrummy Castle Hotel, Nr Alford

Outstanding baronial home with a magnificent stairway. The hotel blends colonial-like extravagance with eiderdown comfort. Here, you feel like a millionaire's best friend. Fine food and a wine list that spans the globe adds up to a grand Aberdeenshire experience. ❧ Map D5 • (01975) 571288 • www. kildrummycastlehotel.co.uk • ££££

4 Culloden House, Inverness

Bonnie Prince Charlie stayed here (he commandeered the place in 1746) and the hosts have dined out on the story ever since. Glistening chandeliers and Adams plasterwork enhance a building of exceptional architecture. Every room uniquely decorated, and superb dining. ❧ Map D4 • (01463) 790461 • www.culloden house.co.uk • ££££

5 Balfour Castle, Orkney

An extraordinary retreat, its hospitality overseen by the remarkable Zawadskis (see p45). ❧ Shapinsay • Map A5 • (01856) 711282 • www. balfourcastle.co.uk • £££

6 Shieldhill Castle, Biggar

Established in 1199, this venerable castle offers undiluted comfort ... as well as over 90 malts in the Gun Room Bar. Eat à la carte or more cheaply in the Armoury, where the chef's experimental dishes are offered. ❧ Map G5 • (01899) 220035 • www. shieldhill.co.uk • £££

7 Knockinaam Lodge, Portpatrick

A twisting road leads to this romantic setting, within calling distance of the sea. A refined establishment whose charges include dinner and breakfast (see pp83). ❧ Map H3 • (01776) 810471 • ££££

8 Ednam House Hotel, Kelso

Classic Georgian mansion, with an outlook over the River Tweed – a major draw for its rooms and classy restaurant. The building retains period features and, though slightly heavy-handed with patterns, its clutter of fishing paraphernalia adds a homely feel. ❧ Map G6 • (01573) 224168 • www.ednam house.com • £££

9 Glenfinnan House Hotel, Glenfinnan

An imposing 18th-century pine-panelled stately home which overlooks Loch Shiel. Excellent value, the rooms ranging in price according to views, this hotel has good home cooking and a bar where folk musicians often gather. ❧ Map E3 • (01397) 722235 • £££

10 Easter Dunfallandy Country House, Pitlochry

In a tranquil location overlooking the Tummel valley, this small country house has just six bedrooms. Voted into the top 20 B&Bs for the whole of Britain, Easter Dunfallandy is inexpensive rural living, where the day begins with a hearty Highland breakfast. No children under 12 are allowed, no dogs ... and no risk of disturbance to the tranquillity. ❧ Map E4/5 • (01796) 474128 • www.dunfallandy. co.uk • ££

www.celticcastles.com provides an on-line booking service for castles with accommodation throughout Scotland

Price Categories

For a standard, double room per night (with breakfast if included), taxes and extra charges.

£	under £50
££	£50–100
£££	£100–150
££££	£150–200
£££££	over £200

Left **Ivybank Guest House** Right **Woodston Fishing Station**

Mainland Guest Houses and B&Bs

1 Ivybank Guest House, Inverness

In her home of immense charm Catherine Cameron runs an exceptional open house, which honours the finest tradition of Highland hospitality. Great comfort, run of her library and a relaxing sense of freedom are what make a stay here so memorable. ◎ 28 Old Edinburgh Rd • Map D4 • (01463) 232796 • ££

2 Little Fordel, Melrose

Close to the abbey in a quiet cul-de-sac, this B&B is a friendly home, fully supportive of all a traveller's needs: warmth, shelter and a hearty breakfast. It even arranges transfer lifts for walkers and has a drying room in the unlikely event of rain! ◎ Abbey St • Map G5 • (01896) 822206 • £

3 Woodston Fishing Station, St Cyrus

Up above St Cyrus beach, this guest house comprises a huddle of historic buildings. The Fishing Station was established in 1826 and to it was added a Victorian villa and vaulted ice house, all now providing splendid accommodation at unbeatable rates. ◎ Map E6 • (01674) 850226 • www.woodston fishingstation.co.uk • ££

4 Port-na-Con, Loch Eriboll

Within a pebble toss of the sea, Port-na-Con is a former Customs House built over 200 years ago. Cosy rooms (only three) and a conservatory overlooking Loch Eriboll. Children-friendly, and a scrumptious restaurant (see p129). ◎ Loch Eriboll, Nr Durness • Map B4 • (01971) 511367 • ££

5 Old Pines, Spean Bridge

This restaurant-with-rooms is a Scandinavian-style house with a "Best Small Hotel in Britain" award. Single-storey, easy wheelchair access, play area for children and views to Ben Nevis through the lovely pine trees. Dinner (by Master Chef Suki Barber) included with accommodation (see p115). ◎ Map E3 • (01397) 712324 • www.oldpines.co.uk • ££££

6 Kinkell House, Cromarty Firth

A delightful country house, which catches the sunrise over the Cromarty Firth and the sunset over Ben Wyvis. Furnished and decorated with an aesthete's eye, this relaxing home is outstanding value, with a fine à la carte menu each evening. ◎ Conor Br, Nr Dingwall • Map C/D4 • (01349) 861270 • ££

7 Dunduff House, Ayrshire

This imposing farmhouse with a stately round tower overlooks the sea and is gazed upon by shaggy Highland cattle. A fine B&B that welcomes all, except smokers and pets. ◎ Dunure, on coast road between Ayr and Culzean Castle • Map G3/4 • (01292) 500225 • www. gemmelldunduff.co.uk • ££

8 Newton of Nydie Farmhouse, St Andrews

A stone-built farmhouse seven minutes' drive from St Andrews. Surrounded by wheatfields, it is a spacious home with a private lounge and chairs you can disappear into. Huge breakfasts; non-smoking. ◎ Map F5 • (01334) 850204 • ££

9 The Famous Bein Inn, Glenfarg

Originally a drover's inn dating back 140 years, this hostelry fulfils its claim of being "a little bit different". Flower-bedecked and slightly kitsch on the exterior, inside its bar is a temple to rock music. Live "unplugged" sessions make this a unique place to eat, drink and (possibly) sleep. ◎ Glenfarg, Perth • Map E5 • (01577) 830216 • www.beininn.com • ££

10 Arkaig Guest House, Aberdeen

Built in Aberdeen granite, this family-run guest-house is only 10 minutes' walk from the city centre. Full breakfast included; dinners by arrangement and all rooms have TVs and phones. Patio garden to relax in at the back. ◎ 43 Powis Ter, Aberdeen • Map D6 • (01224) 638872 • www.arkaig.biz • £

Note: Unless otherwise stated, all hotels accept credit cards and have en-suite bathrooms

Left **Northbay House** Centre **Cuin Lodge** Right **Ardhasaig**

Island Guesthouses and B&Bs

1 Glenmachrie Farmhouse, Islay

This working farm is also a wildlife sanctuary and eco-conscious zone. Alasdair and Rachel Whyte are tending their corner of the planet, and to share their home is to experience comfort, hospitality, organic food and, of course, natural harmony. ◊ *Port Ellen • Map G2 • (01496) 302560 • ££*

2 Northbay House, Barra

A sparklingly modern guesthouse, converted from a schoolhouse close to Barra's famous beaches. Laundry facilities, packed lunches and wheelchair access, too. Non-smoking; no pets. Only two bedrooms, but self-catering also possible. ◊ *Map D1 • (01871) 890255 • £*

3 Kirkapol Guest House, Tiree

Through lancet windows, this converted church gives views over Hawaii-like stretches of beach. A quiet repose on this beautiful island, with simple en-suite rooms and dinners available by request. ◊ *Gott Bay, Scarnish • Map E1 • (01879) 220729 • www.kirkapol tiree.co.uk • ££*

4 Glen Cloy Farmhouse, Arran

Lovely ivy-clad home in a peaceful glen just outside Brodick. A short distance away are the castle, golf course and paths to Goat

Fell. Homemade shortbread and preserves, eggs from runabout hens and other healthy farm produce. ◊ *Glen Cloy Rd, Brodick • Map G3 • (01770) 302351 • www.Smooth Hound.co.uk/hotels/ glencloy.html • ££*

5 College of the Holy Spirit, Isle of Cumbrae

Overnight or weekly accommodation in a historic college adjoining Britain's smallest cathedral, the Cathedral of the Isles. Full and half board available, depending on the current programme. A timeless and deeply spiritual place to rest mind and body. ◊ *Firth of Clyde • Map F/G3 • (01475) 530353 • www. argyll.anglican.org • £*

6 Park View Guest House, Shetland

This fine old stone house, with tennis courts and seafront shops nearby, has a prime, quiet location and offers all home comforts. Ideal accommodation anytime, but especially good for the Up Helly Aa festival *(see p37).* ◊ *68a St Olaf Street, Lerwick • Map B2 • (01595) 692671 • £*

7 Quivals, Orkney

The small island of Sandsay is a gem, and Mrs Flett runs a superb guesthouse here in her traditional house. She welcomes children and pets and caters for special diets. A native Orcadian

upholding the islanders' tradition of hospitality. ◊ *Sanday • Map A5/6 • (01857) 600467 • £*

8 Cuin Lodge, Mull

The Aitkens have turned this 19th-century shooting lodge into a lovely guesthouse, set in peaceful countryside outside the village of Dervaig. Panoramic views of Loch Cuin and Ben More, and good home cooking for an evening meal. ◊ *Dervaig • Map E2 • (01688) 400346 • www.cuin-lodge @mull.com • £*

9 Tables Hotel, Skye

Wonderful little guesthouse with resident dog (Max) beside the peat fire. Cosy rooms looking out over the sea loch to flat-topped hills, MacLeod's Tables. Plenty of atmosphere in the bar and very friendly service. Good food too. ◊ *Dunvegan • Map D2 • (01470) 521404 • www.tables-hotel.co.uk • ££*

10 Ardhasaig House, Isle of Harris

Set by one of the most picturesque roads in the isles, this 1904 house has been completely refurbished, while retaining certain period features. Light décor, simple furnishings, captivating views – a B&B of the highest calibre, with the option of dinner. A self-catering cottage is also available. ◊ *Ardhasaig • Map C2 • (01859) 502066 • ££*

Price Categories

For a standard,	**£** under £50
double room per	**££** £50–100
night (with breakfast	**£££** £100–150
if included), taxes	**££££** £150–200
and extra charges.	**£££££** over £200

Left **Carbisdale Castle** Right **Rowardennan**

🏆 Youth Hostels and Camp Sites

1 Carbisdale Castle Youth Hostel, Culrain

Where your home is your castle. Scotland's most magnificent hostel and one that should not be missed (see p63). 🔹 Map C4 • (01549) 421232 • £

2 Lochranza Youth Hostel, Arran

In a beautiful situation below Arran's mountains, close to the sea and an ancient castle, rests Lochranza Hostel. Secluded in a woodland garden, this old country house makes a great base for exploring the island. Close to a bus route and with its own small shop. 🔹 Lochranza • Map G3 • (01770) 830631 • 1 Mar–26 Oct • £

3 Sands Holiday Centre, Gairloch

Beside a pristine length of beach, this grassy caravan site has a prime location. The Cameron family are low on rules and high on visitor enjoyment. Camp, caravan or hire a wooden sheiling (hut). The splendours of Torridon, Inverewe and Loch Maree are nearby. 🔹 Map C3 • (01445) 712152 • www.highlandcaravan camping.co.uk • £

4 Coldingham Hostel, Eyemouth

If you're into surfing or kayaking, this is the place. But even if you're not, the views across sand and surf are truly exhilarating, and there's plenty of good walking. Plain hostel in a red stone building – but what a setting! 🔹 Coldingham Sands, Eyemouth • Map F6 • 22 Mar–28 Sep • (01890) 771298 • £

5 Glenfinnan Sleeping Car, Glenfinnan

The most unusual beds in Scotland are to be found in a railway sleeping coach, which has ceased rolling and now stands at Glenfinnan Station Museum. Sleeps ten, and you can pay by the night or hire the whole wagon by the week. All-day light meals served in adjacent coach. 🔹 Glenfinnan Station Museum • Map E3 • (01397) 722295 • £

6 The Burgh Lodge, Falkland

Accommodation for 36 is provided here, and you choose: backpacker dormitory, two twin rooms, four family, and two for disabled. Set in the centre of this lovely village and with super views of the Lomond hills from the roundel. Very friendly and cheap. Bed linen supplied and free hot drinks. 🔹 Back Wynd • Map F5 • (01337) 857710 • £

7 Rowardennan Youth Hostel, nr Drymen

One of the busiest youth hostels because of its location: on the banks of Loch Lomond and also on the West Highland Way walking path (see p42). Ben Lomond sweeps up at the back and at the front is a private beach. Very popular with families, so book ahead. 🔹 Map F4 • 1 Mar–26 Oct • (01360) 870259 • £

8 Berneray Youth Hostel, Berneray

Thatched cottage providing primitive accommodation in the most stunning situation. Just four hops to the beach (see p45). 🔹 North Uist • Map C1 • www.gatliff. org.uk • £

9 Kinloch Castle, Rum

If you find yourself near Rum, make a beeline for this incredible hostel – the castle and island defy all descriptions. It's sure to be an experience to conjure reminiscences in years to come (see pp44–5). 🔹 Map D2 • (01687) 462037 • £

10 Sandyhills Bay Leisure Park, Kirkcudbright

A grassy patch, with 30 pitches for caravans or tents, a beach of its own and an adjacent golf course. Spotless amenities, a licensed shop and take-away snacks are all sources of pride to the owners, the Gillespie family. Spectacular walks and smugglers' caves nearby. 🔹 Map H4 • (01557) 870267 • www. gillespie-leisure.co.uk • £

General Index

Special Editions

Top 10 Guides can be purchased in bulk quantities at discounted prices. Personalized jackets and excerpts can also be tailored to meet your needs.

Please contact (in the UK) – Sarah.Burgess@dk.com or Special Sales, Dorling Kindersley Ltd, 80 Strand, London WC2R 0RL; (in the US) – Special Markets Department, DK Publishing, Inc., 375 Hudson Street, New York, NY 10014.

Acknowledgments

The Author
Alastair Scott is a freelance travel writer and photographer based in Edinburgh and on the Isle of Skye.

Produced by
BLUE ISLAND PUBLISHING
Editorial Director Rosalyn Thiro
Art Director Stephen Bere
Associate Editor Michael Ellis
Designers Lee Redmond, Ian Midson
Picture Research Ellen Root
Proofreader & indexer Jane Simmonds
Fact Checker Sheena Scott

Photographer Linda Whitwam
Additional Photography Peter Anderson, Joe Cornish, Steve Gorton, Paul Harris, Dave King, Roger Phillips, Clive Streeter and Stephen Whitehorn
Cartography James McDonald, Mapping Ideas Ltd

AT DORLING KINDERSLEY
Publisher Douglas Amrine
Senior Art Editor Marisa Renzullo
Senior Cartographic Editor Casper Morris; **Senior DTP** Jason Little
Production Controller Melanie Dowland

Picture Credits
Dorling Kindersley would like to thank all the churches, museums, hotels, restaurants, bars and other sights for their assistance and kind permission to photograph.

Placement Key: t=top; tl=top left; tr= top right; tc=top centre; tcl=top centre left; c=centre; cr=center right; b=bottom; bl=bottom left; br=bottom right.

ARDHASAIG: 150tr.
BABBITY BOWSTER: 146tl; BALMORAL: 142tl; BOATH HOUSE: 147tr; BRIDGE-MAN ART LIBRARY: Private Col.: 32t. Laurie Campbell: 7cb, 7c, 40tr, 52b, 125t; CELTIC CASTLES: 148tl, 148tc; CORBIS: Nathan Benn 28-9; Niall Benvie 122tl; Franz-Marc Frei 78tr; WildCountry 122tr; CUIN LODGE: 150tc; CULLODEN HOUSE: 148tr.
DK IMAGES: Science Museum 34b. Mary Evans Picture library: 32tl, 32tc, 32c, 33tr.
ANDREW FAIRLIE: 89tl.

GLASGOW MUSEUMS: Burrell Collection 16b, 16-7, 17t; GLASGOW SCIENCE CENTRE: 19cb; Ashley Coombes 6b, 18b, 19b; Owen Edelsten 19t, 19ca; Keith Hunter 18–9; GLASGOW TOURIST OFFICE: 18t, 18c, 36tl, 93tr.
DENNIS HARDLEY: 20t, 21b, 26t, 26b, 27c, 40tl, 42tl, 50tl, 111b, 116cl, 116cr, 117b; PAUL HARRIS: 4–5, 25t, 31t.
ISLE OF ERISKA HOTEL: 147tl;
IVYBANK GUEST HOUSE: 149tl.
MULL THEATRE: 123tr.
NATIONAL GALLERY OF SCOTLAND: 6ca; all 12–13; © TRUSTEES OF THE NATIONAL MUSUEMS OF SCOTLAND: 6cb, all 14-5, 69b; NATIONAL TRUST FOR SCOTLAND: 7b, 28t, 28c, 29t, 29b; G.A. Day 103b; Douglas MacGregor 28b; Harvey Wood 29c, 94tc. NORTHBAY HOUSE: 150tl.
PA PHOTOS: 33bl, 33cl, 34tr; PEAT INN: 89tl; POINT HOTEL: Andrew Doolan Architects 143tr; PORT-NA-CON: 138tl.
IAN SARGEANT: 22b, 22tl, 117t; ALAS-TAIR SCOTT: 20-1, 25b, 27b, 31b, 38tl, 40b, 45b, 46c, 52tl, 57t, 62tl, 62tr, 62b, 63t, 63b, 99b, 126b, 127tl, 128b; SCOT-TISH NATIONAL GALLERY OF MODERN ART: 71tl; SCOTTISH YHA: 141tl, 151tl/tr; SHETLAND ISLES TOURISM: 37br, 124tc, 124tl, 129; ST JUDES: 145. STILL MOVING PICTURES: 125b; Jason Baxter 58tl; Anne Burgess 30t; Richard Campbell 116t; Doug Corrance 37tl, 44c, 58tr, 59t, 59c, 60tr, 60b, 119b, 124c; Mark Ferguson 124tr, 124b, 126t, 128tl, 128tr; John Guidi 113br; Angus Johnston 22tr, 24b, 26-7, 27t, 92b; Derek Laird 23, 70; Robert Lees 41t, 118b; Henry McInnes 118t; Ken Patterson 36b, 36c, 53t; Mark Pepper 64tr; David Robertson 44t, 119l; Glyn Satterley 37tr; S J Taylor 8–9, 36tc, Harvey Wood 36tr, 45t.
THE TOWER: 64b, 77tr;
THREE CHIMNEYS: 123tl.
THE WITCHERY BY THE CASTLE: 64tl, 77tl, 142tr; WOODSTON FISHING STATION: 149tr.

JACKET
Front: DK IMAGES: clb; Steve Gorton bl; Roger Phillips tc; Stephen Whitehorne cla; GETTY IMAGES: Kathy Collins main image.
Back: DK IMAGES: Joe Cornish tl; Stephen Whitehorne tc, tr.

Index of Main Streets